GW00801973

BRANNON'S

# PICTURE

OF

# The Isle of Wight

OR

*The Expeditious Travellers*

## INDEX

*To its premier of Beauty & Variety, So....*

*The Pulpit Rock, Bonchurch, looking towards Ventnor*

*Compiled especially with Reference to those numerous Visitors who can spare but two or three Days,*

TO MAKE THE

## Tour of the Island.

*Printed and Published by George Brannon, Wootton.*
ISLE OF WIGHT.

Brannon's Picture of The Isle of Wight
or the The Expeditious Traveller's Index
To its Prominent Beauties & Objects of Interest.
Compiled especially with Reference to those numerous
Visitors who can spare but two or three Days
to make the
Tour of the Island.
Printed and Published by George Brannon, Wootton,

ISLE OF WIGHT.

# EXPLANATION.

If nearly FORTY YEARS' RESIDENCE in the Isle of Wight may be allowed in some degree to qualify an ARTIST for the office of Guide, the Author has a fair claim to public patronage,—for few could have had better opportunity of acquiring local information.

He has endeavoured to render THE PICTURE an intelligent *Cicerone*, without being too garrulous or grandiloquous,—but always attentive to the stranger, leading him to every remarkable object, and giving just as much description of each, as would be acceptable to persons enjoying the full use of their eyes. It affords him, *at first glance*, an INDEX of what ought to be seen, and *how best seen in the shortest time*, in every place to which he may be successively conducted. This novelty in the work will prove very frequently of great utility, especially to those visitors who have too little time for their trip, and who, for want of such a laconic memento wherever they go, are known in a thousand instances to pass by the most interesting objects unnoticed,—not being aware even of their proximity.

This being the production of the same hand as several other local works, it is due to the stranger to explain in what respects they differ:—

I.—THE VECTIS SCENERY is a handsome volume in Royal Quarto, substantially bound, containing 36 highly finished line-engravings of all the most celebrated landscapes, accompanied with ample letter-press descriptions, price £1.5.0.

II.—THE PICTURE differs from the above in being intended for a *hand-book*, it is in fact a Cicerone, and therefore occasionally dwells with a degree of minuteness which could be interesting only to a person actually on the spot; but the "Vectis Scenery" takes the higher rank of an Exhibitor of picturesque scenes which ask little aid from verbal explanation, and is entitled to a place on the drawing-room table with other works of Art. The Engravings in the two publications are quite different.

III.—The PLEASURE-VISITOR'S COMPANION is a compendium of useful information, with the different Tours, &c. and Views of the Country Inns, price 2s., or with Map, 3s.

IV.—The REV. LEGH RICHMOND'S DESCRIPTION of the Island, with explanatory Notes and illustrative Engravings, price 2s.6d.

V.—A MAP of the Island and the Opposite Coast—with the Tours, &c., in cover, price 1s.6d.

It were useless to complain of the piracies committed upon the Author's labors, both literary and pictorial, by parties in London as well as in the country; but he may be allowed however to remark, that some of the most common facts and delineations are strangely perverted from the Truth in their new dress,—however artfully disguised to prevent the consequences of palpable detection.

In cases even where a professional Author may be engaged by a publisher on a local work, the time allowed is generally too limited for acquiring accurate knowledge of his subjects: he must depend either on prior publications or on his personal intercourse with the residents, for much of his information. In compiling from the first of these sources, he is very liable to mis-statement, by investing everything in a new dress to conceal his piracies; and the latter source leaves him open to imposition—for much of his matter will be sheer gossip, partial statements, or unfounded tradition, which a long experience only could detect, and place in a proper light.

NORRIS CASTLE

# CONTENTS.

CHAPTER IV.—THE SOUTH-WESTERN COAST OF THE ISLAND,

*Distinguished for the most Sublime Scenery.*
The Road over the Downs to Freshwater
Freshwater Cliffs, Bay, and Caverns
High-down, Main-bench, and Scratchell's Bay
Needle Rocks, Alum Bay, Light-house, &c.
Freshwater Village, Yarmouth, Calbourne, &c.

Conspicuous Objects on the Hills
Tours through, and Voyage round the Island
Lists of the Inns and Seats. Passage and Conveyance, &c.

# LIST OF THE ENGRAVINGS.

# CHAPTER I.

## THE PECULIAR ADVANTAGES OF THE ISLAND AS THE OBJECT OF

## A SUMMER'S EXCURSION.

Variety is the characteristic charm of the Isle of Wight; the scenery being in fact a most happy combination of the grand and romantic, the sylvan and marine—throughout a close interchange of hills and dales, intersected by streams and rivers: combining the quiet of rural life with the fashionable gaiety of a watering-place, or the bustle of a crowded sea-port. But generally, its landscapes are more distinguished for beauty than sublimity, and hence the very appropriate designation of "THE GARDEN OF ENGLAND!" an emphatic compliment cheerfully paid by the thousands annually visiting its shores for pleasure or for health: and perhaps there is scarcely another spot in the kingdom, of the same narrow limits, which can concentrate more of those qualities that at once charm the eye and animate the soul. Nor should it be overlooked how large a source of interest is derived from the proximity of those two celebrated towns, Southampton and Portsmouth: and the beautiful termination given to most of the open prospects by the retiring distances on the opposite coast.

> — —"Intermixture sweet,
> Of lawns and groves, of open and retired,
> Vales, farms, towns, villas, castles, distant spires.
> And hills on hills with ambient clouds enrolled,
> In long succession court the lab'ring sight."

But the crowning beauty of the Island is certainly THE SEA! viewed in all the splendor of its various aspects;—whether under the awful grandeur of the agitated and boundless *Ocean*,—as a rapid and magnificent *River*,—or reposing in all the glassy tranquillity of a spacious land-locked *Bay*:—now of a glowing crimson, and now of

1

the purest depth of azure: its bosom ever spangled with a thousand moving and attractive objects of marine life.

To those who have never had the opportunity of viewing the sea except under the comparatively dreary aspect which it presents from many unsheltering parts of the southern coast, as for instance Brighton, where almost the only relief to the monotony of the wide expanse is a few clumsy fishing boats or dusky colliers, and occasionally the rolling clouds of smoke from a passing steamer,—it may seem that we are rather disposed to exaggerate the picture; but not so, as would certainly be attested by every one who had visited the island: for here the scene is ever enriched by magnificent SHIPS OF WAR, innumerable merchant-vessels, and splendid pleasure-yachts, safely lying at anchor or gaily sailing about in every direction; and what moving object in the world can surpass, in grandeur, beauty, and interest, a fine ship under full canvass with a light breeze? Let the reader only imagine how glorious a sight it must have been, when 200 sail,—line-of-battle-ships, frigates, and large merchantmen under convoy, would weigh anchor at the same time, and proceeding on their voyage, *pass round the island* as it were in review!—thus affording a spectacle, as they floated

"O'er the glad waters of the dark blue sea,"

never to be erased from the memory of those who had once the incomparable pleasure to witness it. True it is, that in these happier times of peace, such exhibitions are not to be expected: but frequently even now, very large fleets of merchantmen, and perhaps several men-of-war, which have put in through distress of weather, or been detained by contrary winds, will all at the same moment weigh anchor at the first favorable change. [Footnote: The glories of the olden time have of late years been frequently revived at the departure of Experimental and other squadrons rendezvousing at Spithead,—accompanied as they sometimes are by hundreds of sailing-craft and steamers, including the beautiful yachts of all the neighbouring clubs.]

We think it ridiculous to attribute qualities to the island (as is often done,) which it really does not possess: all we contend for is, that few spots can excel the Wight *altogether in the amount of its* VARIOUS *attractions*; we mean especially to those parties who can only snatch occasionally a very brief period for a summer excursion; not only as regards its *peculiar and acknowledged local advantages*, but equally so from those adventitious and auxiliary circumstances that are derived from the present *rail-road* conveyance from the metropolis: and from the *shortness* and *perfect safety* of the passage across—being little more than an hour from Southampton, and only half that time from Portsmouth; the former an important mercantile port and fashionable watering-place; and the latter, the first naval station in the kingdom—its marine treasures too thrown open gratuitously to public inspection: and what curiosity can afford a Briton more gratification, than to visit such a dock-yard, and pace the deck of the very ship in which *Victory* crowned the last moments of the immortal Nelson?

Though the island has to boast of many passages of highly romantic and *brilliant* scenery, yet the predominant character of its landscapes is, as was hinted above, calculated to amuse, to delight, and promote *cheerfulness*, rather than to astonish or impress the spectator with feelings of awe by their stupendous grandeur; circumstances which, combined with its salubrity of climate, render it a most desirable retreat to the valetudinarian and nervous invalid: indeed all the alterations which have latterly been made, or are now in progress, tend to soften, embellish, and in point of convenience to improve the face of the country. On this subject however it will be a question with many persons of good taste, whether any of these artificial operations are really improvements upon the native character of the island. An artist would most probably decide in the negative: but we know there are many nevertheless, who consider that whatever deterioration the island may experience in some of her more wild and romantic features, is amply compensated by the spread of cultivation and rural decoration, by the increased facilities of travelling, and the multiplied means of enjoyment now afforded to the pleasure-tourist.

A few particulars will suffice for the present, to prove the above assertions, and may perhaps be found

### USEFUL HINTS TO STRANGERS

Purposing a visit to the shores of the Garden of England. They may arrange to breakfast comfortably at the usual hour in London—start by the rail-road, and reach either of the above ports at noon, or even earlier—steam-packets are in readiness to convey the passengers across, and stage-coaches and other vehicles await their arrival at Cowes and Ryde: our friends may then *ride round one-half* of the island, and return the next, or even *the same night!* but this of course is abridging the affair a little too much. But allow a full week, and that will suffice to render it a very pleasant trip. If, for example, you come to Southampton, sleep there, or at least tarry a few hours in the examination of it: then take the last steamer to Cowes or Ryde, and sleep there the first night: next morning commence the regular Tour of three days, dining and sleeping twice or thrice at one or other of the inns situated on the rocky side of the island, to enjoy at the same time the more unusual feast of a wide prospect of the sea, and the music of the foaming breakers thundering on the beach below. Supposing you start from Cowes, as being opposite Southampton, the Route will bring you round to Ryde; where you cross to Portsmouth, and having gone over the fortifications, the dock-yard, and Nelson's ship, return by one or other of the rail-roads. But if you arrive by Portsmouth and Ryde, then return *via* Cowes and 'Hampton.—For the details of the several routes, the reader is of course referred to the chapter "Tours," at the end of the Work.

That part of the island immediately opposite Hampshire is generally well-wooded, with an easy descent to the shore—populous and busy, as might be expected from the two considerable watering-places before named, and several excellent harbors. But the south side (familiarly called *the Back of the Island*,) being washed by the impetuous tides of the ocean, presents a very different aspect, showing the resistless progress of the waves:—and hence perpendicular cliffs of great altitude, precipitous slopes constantly detaching large masses of earth and rocks, and all the picturesque confusion produced by successive landslips: here therefore the scenery is variously characterized by dreary devastation, romantic beauty, or sublime splendor of effect. But not so of *the Interior* of the island, which presents the softer pictures of pastoral and rural life: for ...

"Creation's mildest charms are here combined,"

enlivened by several splendid mansions, with their parks and groves. The churches are numerous: some "embosomed soft in trees," and others picturesquely seated on commanding knolls: and many of the highest hills are adorned by a light-house or signal-station—some lofty obelisk, tower, or mill; so that in every direction a conspicuous object gives an interest and discriminative identity to those broad features of scenery, which would otherwise be perfectly tame and monotonous.

*Situation, Extent, Climate, &c.*

The Isle of Wight extends from east to west 23 miles, by about 14 from north to south (being very nearly the figure of a lozenge), circumscribes at least 60 miles, and contains upwards of 100,000 acres. It is separated from the Hampshire coast by a strait called the SOLENT SEA, varying from three to seven miles in width: and bounded by the British Channel on the south—the nearest part of the French coast being Cherbourg (18 leagues distant), which is said to have been seen from the hills of Freshwater, &c. The extent of the English coast visible in clear weather is above 100 miles, from Beachy Head in Sussex, to the Isle of Portland in Dorset.

THE CLIMATE.—The purity of the air was always acknowledged by those who ever visited the island owing to the dry and highly cultivated face of the country: but it was left to an eminent Physician, Dr. James Clarke, to give due celebrity to the unrivaled salubrity of the climate:—

"The Island, from the variety which it presents in point of elevation, soil, and aspect, and from the configuration of its hills and shores, possesses several peculiarities of climate and situation, which render it a very favorable and commodious residence throughout the year, for a large class of invalids. On this account, the Isle of Wight claims our particular attention, as it comprehends within itself advantages which are of great value to the delicate invalid, and to obtain which, in almost any other part of England, he would require to make a considerable journey." And he further remarks, that "the Undercliff bids fair to exceed all other winter residences in this country, and the island will have added to its title of the Garden of England, that of the BRITISH MADEIRA."

The classical designation of the island is VECTA or VECTIS: but its modern name is derived from Wect, With, or Wict, as it is found variously written in Doomsday Book.

Some writers have supposed the island to have been once connected with the mainland by an isthmus stretching from Gurnet, near Cowes, to Leap, on the Hampshire roast; but nothing decisive has yet been advanced in support of this strange hypothesis.

The surface of the island presents a constant succession of valley and eminence—the two principal chains of hills being ... a range of chalk downs of a smooth rounded shape, and from 500 to 700 feet high, that stretch lengthways through the middle of the island, abutting the ocean at Freshwater on the west, and Bembridge on the east:-and a still loftier range, variously composed of chalk, firestone, &c., that skirts the south-eastern coast from Shanklin Down to St. Catharine's (the latter 830 feet in height,) and whose broken flank on the sea-side forms the celebrated and romantic region of the UNDERCLIFF.

The principal streams in the Isle of Wight navigable for marine craft are the Rivers Medina and Yar, and the Creeks of Newtown and Wootton.—The Medina, whose source is in the south, and which joins the sea at Cowes, divides the island into two hundreds of nearly equal extent, respectively called the East and West Medene; the first comprising 14, the latter 16 parishes.

The population of the island has doubled since 1802, and now exceeds 45,000. No manufacture of any consequence is carried on (with the exception of the lace-factory near Newport,) Corn being the staple article of trade,—for which there are about 42 mills, nearly all of them worked by water.

Almost encompassed by formidable rocks and shelves, few parts of the English coast are more dangerous to ships driving in a storm. The most dreaded parts are the Needles and Shingles, at the western point; Rocken-end Race at the south, and Bembridge Ledge at the eastern extremity: few winters pass without the melancholy catastrophe of shipwreck; though the danger is now of course diminished by the establishment of Light-houses—especially of the new one near Niton.—Owing to this cause, and to the precipitous nature of the coast itself, the island presents few points favorable to an enemy's landing, and even those were for the most part fortified by order of Henry VIII: The forts of Sandown, Cowes, and Yarmouth still remain; and though they might be of little use in the present state of military science, the presence of "England's wooden walls" at the stations of Spithead and St. Helen's, renders all local defences needless.

*Geology, Agriculture, and Zoology.*

The island presents many rare geological phenomena: and from its smallness, easy access, and the various nature of its coasts, offers an admirable field for scientific investigation.

One peculiarity deserves to be particularly noticed; namely, the extraordinary state in which the FLINTS are found in the great range of chalk hills,—for all those in regular beds, are broken into pieces in every direction, from two or three inches long, to an almost impalpable powder; and yet show no other indication of their fracture than very fine lines, until the investing chalk be removed, when they fall at once to pieces! But the separate flints or nodules in the body of the chalk strata are not so: which led the late Sir H. Englefield to conjecture, that the phenomenon was caused in the moment of the immense concussion which subverted the whole mass of strata, and placed them in their present nearly vertical position.

Another interesting circumstance in the geological structure of the Isle of Wight, is a series of strata, *vertical* or highly inclined, which run across the middle of it from east to west; while the strata on each side are *horizontal*; they consist of ... a very thick stratum of clay and sand (observable at Alum Bay), flinty chalk, chalk without flints, chalk-marle, green sandstone with lime-stone and chert, dark-grey marle, and ferruginous sand.

A PROGRESSIVE CHANGE is evidently taking place in the boundary line of the coast—the sea making considerable invasions on the south side, which is exposed to the resistless currents of the ocean; while on the north it is found to be more gradually receding, from the accumulation of sand and shingle drifted and deposited by the less impetuous tides of the Solent Channel.—About Brixton, for instance, between Blackgang Chine and the Freshwater Cliffs, the loss of land has been estimated (from the successive removals of paths and hedges,) to exceed 200 feet in breadth in less than a century; while in the neighbourhood of Ryde it is known that the bed of a valley formerly accessible to the sea is now rather above its highest level; and even in 1760, when Fielding visited the island, the coast there is described by him as a wide disgusting waste of mud, which is now covered with an increasing layer of sand, sufficiently firm to bear wheel-carriages; and no doubt but in process of time there will be a great accession to the beach, from the constant though slow operation of the same causes—denuding on the one side, and reciprocally accumulating on the other.

Good Stone of various qualities is found in most parts of the island: and with that procured from the quarries of Binstead, the body of Winchester Cathedral was built. All the houses along the Undercliff are constructed with a beautiful kind of freestone procured on the spot.

Extensive pits are worked in the downs for the chalk, which is used for manure, burning into lime, &c. A stratum of coals was formerly believed to run through the central downs, and Sir Rt. Worsley actually sunk a shaft for it near Bembridge; his labors however were but poorly rewarded. Veins of coarse iron ore have also appeared in some parts of the island.

The finest white sand in the kingdom is obtained from the sea-cliffs at Freshwater, and is carried in great quantities to the glass and porcelain manufactories. Excellent brick-earth abounds in almost every part of the island: common native alum, copperas, specimens of petrifactions, and many curious varieties of sea-weeds, are picked up on the shores; in the cliffs and quarries are found numerous beautiful fossil remains,—especially oysters and other bivalve shells, of a vast size.

The central range of chalk hills divides the island into two nearly distinct regions, the soil and strata being essentially different,—a stiff clay predominating on the north side, which is extensively covered with wood, while the south side is principally of a light sandy soil or mellow loam, and being exceedingly fertile, the whole tract is almost exclusively employed in tillage.

In geological terms, the north is formed of the *Eocene* or freshwater deposits: and the south of the *Cretaceous* or oceanic, except where the *Wealden* exhibits itself at Sandown and Brixton bays.—Though affording a great variety of soil, the island is upon the whole well calculated for farming as may be inferred from its proverbial fertility; "it was many years ago computed to produce as much corn in one year as its inhabitants would consume in seven,—and the improved cultivation, with the additional land brought into tillage, has doubtless kept pace with the increased population."

In AGRICULTURE there is now a close approximation to the routine practised in the rest of the county: and there is scarcely any peculiarity observable either in the system of Husbandry, or in the manners of the Yeomanry, who are a very intelligent and respectable class.

The constant intercourse which the inhabitants have with persons from other parts of the kingdom, has in fact erased all insular peculiarities. But the following extract from the Memoirs of Sir John Oglander, which were written about the year 1700, will be read with interest, as exhibiting a most

*Amusing Picture of the Islanders in the 16th century.*

"I have heard," says he, "and partly knowe it to be true, that not only heretofore there was no lawyer nor attorney in owre island, but in Sir George Carey's time [1588] an attorney coming in to settle in the island, was by his command, with a pound of candles hanging att his breech lighted, with bells about his legs, hunted owte of the island; insomuch that owre ancestors lived here so quietly and securely, being neither troubled to London nor Winchester, so they seldom or never went owte of the island; insomuch as when they went to London (thinking it an East India voyage), they always made their wills, supposing no trouble like to travaile."

The extensive downs of the island afford excellent pasture for sheep, whose wool is of a staple not inferior to that produced on the South Downs: and many thousand lambs are annually sent to the London markets. From the improvements effected in Husbandry, there are now nearly sufficient oxen reared and fatted for the use of the inhabitants, instead of the butchers going as formerly, to Salisbury, &c. for their cattle.

The demands of the dock-yards (both here and at Portsmouth,) have greatly thinned the timber of the island, which is principally oak and elm, and is found to grow most luxuriantly in the wooded tract from East Cowes to St. Helen's.

In the time of King Charles II, woods were so extensive, that it is recorded, a squirrel might have run on the tops of the trees from Gurnard to Carisbrooke, and in several other parts for leagues together.

In ZOOLOGY there is nothing very remarkable, except the absence of pole-cats, badgers, and till lately, even foxes: but the poultry-breeders are now indebted for the introduction of the latter to some sparkish amateurs of hunting: many have been killed, but they are still breeding rapidly in the favorable fastnesses of the more rocky and woody districts. Otters too are frequently seen.—GAME is abundant, particular attention having been paid to its preservation. "The great plenty of hares and other game is owing to the care of Sir Edward Horsey, governor in 1582, who is reported to have given a lamb for every living hare brought to him from the neighbouring counties."

THE NIGHTINGALE.—These much-prized birds of passage make the island their early and most favorite resort; and to those visitors from the north who perhaps never heard their unrivaled notes, the opportunity would prove not the least gratifying circumstance in a day's pleasure. On fine evenings in the months of May and June, the woods and groves in every direction resound with the delightful chorus of their inimitable songs.

Astonishing numbers of sea-fowl resort during the summer months to the cliff's of Freshwater and Bembridge: in the latter, the eagle has been known to build its eyry, and in the time of queen Elizabeth they were famous for a breed of hawks, which were so valued, that it was made a capital crime to steal them.

FISH of every kind common to the southern coast of England is caught off the island, but not in that abundance which might be expected, except crabs and lobsters, which are uncommonly large and fine. Mackarel are some seasons extremely plentiful, small, but peculiarly sweet. Numbers of porpoises are seen rolling along in the Solent Sea and Southampton Water; sharks are frequently observed off the back of the island, and sometimes even the grampus pursuing its prey. In 1814, a large whale was taken off the Shingles (west of the Needle Rocks,) having been left aground by the ebbing tide: and in the winter of 1841, another, measuring 75 feet in length, was caught near the same spot.

*Local Biography and History.*

The following are amongst the most eminent natives of the island:

Sir JOHN CHEEKE, Knt., one of the most distinguished scholars and virtuous men of his time: he was tutor to Edward VI, and a zealous protestant, but being induced during the following reign to make a public recantation, his death, which happened soon after, was supposed to have been hastened by shame of that humiliating exhibition.

Rev. HENRY COLE, D.D., Dean of St. Paul's, a contemporary of the above, was born at Godshill: he shone in divinity and literature, and was a strenuous advocate of the Roman-catholic faith.

THOs. JAMES, D.D., a learned divine and antiquary: was esteemed, from his extensive erudition, a living library, Born at Newport, died 1629.

ROBERT HOOK, M.D., celebrated for his extraordinary inventive powers in almost every branch of art and science, was born at Freshwater anno 1635, and died at an advanced age, in Gresham College.

JOHN HOBSON, rose by his skill and courage from the obscurity of a tailor's parish-apprentice to an admiral's rank in the reign of Queen Anne: he headed Sir George Rooke's squadron in the attack on Vigo harbour, where a numerous Spanish fleet was entirely captured or burned.—The little village of Bonchurch claims the honor of his birth-place.

We shall conclude this general chapter with a brief summary of the local history, though the annals of a small dependent isle like this, cannot be expected to possess any very exciting interest.

[In fact it can boast of no important ancient settlements or records—no valued chronicles of the alternate successes and defeats of ambitious rival princes and their contending armies, or the unpitied sufferings of the sacrificed population: and perhaps it would never have been mentioned in the national history, had it not been for the imprisonment of fallen royalty in the case of Charles I. Its situation certainly exposed it to the attacks of Danish pirates, and subsequently of the French; but these distant events constituting but a broken and unconnected narrative, the ensuing brief sketch will we presume be sufficient for the majority of our readers. We refer those who wish further information on the subject to the valuable work of Sir Richard Worsley,—from which this article is partly abridged.]

It was subdued by the Roman troops under Vespasian, A.D. 43; but the conquerors could not have experienced much resistance from the natives, as no remains of their military works have been here discovered. Under the empire, the island was reckoned to contain about 1200 families.

The Saxon kings of the South of England several times attacked the island with their accustomed unsparing ferocity: particularly Cerdic, in 530, who replaced the slaughtered British by a colony of his own countrymen; and Ceadwalla of Murcia, who having seized it in 686, was so incensed at the idolatry of the inhabitants, that he resolved at first to extirpate them, and repeople the island with *Christians!* but at the intercession of bishop Wilfred, great numbers saved their lives by submitting to be baptized.

In the ninth and following centuries the island suffered, in common with the neighbouring coast, from the predatory visits of the Danes. For a time indeed they were checked by the great Alfred, who wholly captured or destroyed one large fleet, laden with the spoils of Hampshire and the Wight: but under the weak and disordered reigns of his successors, the northern pirates seem to have taken possession of this defenceless spot as often as they pleased; and after making it a depot for the plunder of the adjacent counties, and living freely on the inhabitants, sometimes wantonly burned towns and villages at their departure.

The island was also severely harrassed by some of the rebellious Saxon nobles in the reign of Edward the Confessor; but after the Norman Conquest, its tranquillity was not materially disturbed till the year 1346, when a party of French landed at St. Helen's; they were soon repulsed by the islanders, though the warden, Sir Theobald Russell, was amongst the slain. About this time a variety of excellent regulations were made by the inhabitants for their better security: the landholders were by their tenures bound to defend the castle of Carisbrooke for 40 days at their own charges; the county of Devon sent for its defence 76 men-at arms, and the city of London 300 slingers and bowmen.

Another party of the French seem to have made a more successful attack in the first year of Richard II: indeed the islanders at that time had little besides their own valor to depend on for protection; as there were no forts to obstruct an enemy's landing; Carisbrooke Castle standing in the centre of the island, could only serve for a partial retreat: and serious ravages might be committed ere any assistance arrived from the mainland. This want of domestic security so discouraged the natives, that many families withdrew, when an order was issued to the wardens to seize the lands of all such as refused to return.

Not long afterwards a powerful body of Frenchmen landed in the island, the militia of which (900 in number,) had been reinforced from Southampton and London, in expectation of this hostile visit. The invaders were unable to reduce Carisbrooke Castle, which was commanded by the governor, Sir H. Tyrrel—and moreover suffered considerable loss by an ambuscade at a place near Newport, still called Deadman's Lane; [Footnote: A tumulus where the slain were buried, at the south entrance to the town, was exultingly named *Noddies'* Hill—whence the present appellation Nodehill.] yet as the houses of the inhabitants lay at their mercy, they were at length bought off by the payment of 1000 marks, and a promise that no resistance should be offered, if they revisited the island within a year.

In the reign of Henry IV, the French made two other attacks: on the first occasion they were repulsed with loss; and on the second, when a large fleet made a threatening demand of a subsidy, the islanders were so elated at their past success, that they invited the French to land and try their prowess in fair fight, after having had sufficient time to rest and refresh themselves: this handsome challenge was not however accepted.

Owing to its comparatively remote situation, the island escaped those calamities which afflicted the rest of the kingdom during the bloody disputes of the rival Roses: nor was it engaged with any foreign enemy till the year 1488, when the governor, Sir Edward de Woodville, having raised a body of about 500 men, passed over to the continent in aid of the Duke of Bretagne against the king of France. At the battle of St. Aubin the Bretons were routed, and the islanders, whom hatred or contempt of the French probably impelled to a more obstinate resistance, perished to a man: this unfortunate event plunged the whole island into mourning; and in order to recruit the diminished population, an act of parliament forbad any single inhabitant from holding farms above the annual rent of ten marks.

On the 18th of July, 1545, a large French fleet appearing off the Isle of Wight, the English squadron which lay at Spithead, though greatly inferior in force, stood out to meet them: but the admiral's ship *Mary Rose* sinking with most of her crew, the others retreated into the Solent Channel; while the French landed several parties of troops, and after some sharp fighting, repulsed the islanders who had collected to oppose them; it was next proposed in a council of war to fortify and keep possession of the island, but this being considered impracticable by any number of men that could then be spared from the ships, they proceeded to pillage and burn the villages, till the inhabitants, being reinforced, attacked and drove them off with the loss of many men, and one of their principal officers. King Henry VIII, in order to prevent a repetition of such mischievous visits, erected several forts and blockhouses for the protection of the coast; and though the rapid advance of the British naval power still more effectually guarded it from the danger of foreign invasions, the islanders for many years afterwards neglected no precautions for their own defence: a train of field-pieces was provided among the different parishes, and the militia, in 1625, numbered 2000 men.

In the division between king Charles I and the parliament, the islanders at first manifested some zeal in the royal cause; yet as soon as hostilities commenced at Portsmouth, the Newport militia expelled the weak garrison of Carisbrooke Castle, which, with the other forts, were delivered to the parliamentary troops; and on the arrival of the Earl of Pembroke, the gentlemen and principal farmers assembled at Cowes, and tendered him their best services. The inhabitants having thus taken a decisive step in closing with the prevailing power, remained undisturbed spectators of the ensuing commotions, till the king injudiciously sought here an asylum.

On the 12th of November, 1647, Charles, who had just fled from Hampton Court, was met at Tichfield by Colonel Hammond, governor of the Isle of Wight, who invited him to take up his residence at Carisbrooke Castle. The offer was accepted, and for some time the royal guest appeared to be quite free and unrestrained in his actions and company; but afterwards his liberty was gradually abridged, his confidential servants removed, and himself imprisoned within the castle; the various unsuccessful attempts that were made to effect his escape only serving as a pretext to increase the rigor of his confinement. Yet during the subsequent negociations of the Treaty of Newport, he was set at large on his parole,—till a detachment of the army broke off the negociations by arresting and conveying him to Hurst Castle; 30 days before he lost his life at Whitehall.

As its situation preserved it from scenes of hostility between the troops, the island enjoyed a much happier state than any other part of the kingdom during the civil war, which caused many families to retire hither: a circumstance that for the time rose the farm-rents in the proportion of 20 per cent. The subsequent local history presents nothing of any interest, with the exception perhaps of the powerful armaments which assembled in the neighbourhood during the last

French war, and the large bodies of military which were in consequence here quartered.

The absolute lordship of the Isle of Wight was given by William the Conqueror to one William Fitz-Osborne (in reward for his services at the battle of Hastings), "to be held by him as freely as he himself held the realm of England"; but in consequence of the defection of his descendant, it was resumed by the Crown. Henry I granted it to the Earl of Devon, in whose family it long continued, till the alienation of it was obtained by Edward I, for a comparatively small sum. The last grant was to Edward de Woodville in 1485; from which time there have been successively appointed by the Crown,— wardens, captains—and governors of the island: but the powers attached to the office have gradually declined, and at present it is a mere title, unaccompanied by duty or, we believe, emolument.—It is an amusing circumstance in the history of this little spot, that it had once the high-sounding honor of having a *King of its own!*—for the Duke of Warwick was so crowned by the hands of Henry VI, in the year 1444,—but it would seem that the glory of the name was all which his *Vectis* Majesty derived from his accession.

## CHAPTER II.

### Carisbrooke, Newport, Cowes, and Ryde.

As a stranger's attention is frequently diverted from noticing many interesting features of a scene in the hurried moment of his visit, an index 🖙 is placed at the head of each section, pointing only to the *most remarkable objects*—a peculiarity which, it is presumed, will be found extremely useful to those who have little time to spare for minute examination or research.

Our arrangement of the subjects supposes the reader to start from a point nearly central, and pursue his tour of the island in a regular progress, without frequently retrograding, or considerably deviating either to the right or left. This order must prove convenient for reference at all events, let the visitor commence his journey from any of the principal towns.

### CARISBROOKE CASTLE.

CARISBROOKE CASTLE, ISLE OF WIGHT.

"Still farther in the vale a castle lifts
Its stately towers, and tottering battlements,
Drest with the rampant ivy's uncheck'd growth."

☞ *The chief curiosities within the castle are ... THE KEEP, the immense WELL, and the apartments which were the PRISON of King Charles I and his family.*

The high antiquity of this beautiful ruin, which occupies the crown of a hill only one mile westward of Newport, renders it an object of the most pleasing interest with all classes of visitors to the Isle of Wight; and it is the only local specimen of ancient fortification deserving a stranger's notice. It is known to have existed for at least fourteen centuries, having in that long period been subjected of course to many mutations. The Saxon chronicles mention it as a place of strength and importance in the year 530, when Cerdic subdued the island; and it was subsequently rendered almost impregnable, according to the mode of fortification which prevailed among the Normans, by William Fitz-Osborne, to whom the island was given by the Conqueror. And in the reign of queen Elizabeth, it received the most substantial repairs and ample additions; when the outer trenches and bastions were formed upon the plan of those of Antwerp—circumscribing about 20 acres.

On our nearly reaching the top of the hill by the carriage-road, we see first the ancient KEEP, peering above the rest of the ruins; and next, the principal and well-guarded entrance to the interior of the fortress. Passing through an ivied gateway, built in the reign of queen Elizabeth, as appears by the legible inscription (40 E.R. 1520,) on a shield over the arch: we proceed to another gateway in a spacious square building, whose angles are strengthened by two noble round towers: this opens into the interior area; had several prison rooms, and was armed with a portcullis: but the whole of it is now in a sad condition,

Brannon's Picture of the Isle of Wight

"Defac'd by time, and tott'ring in decay!"

Nothing can be more picturesque than the first view of this venerable scene: the most luxuriant ivy everywhere mantles the grey walls and mouldering battlements, interspersed with the waving branches of wild vegetation: and the surrounding terraces are adorned with the opposing tints of pines and every variety of deciduous trees.

Being admitted through the curious old oaken wicket to the inner court, the attendant cicerone will lead the visitor to several objects in due succession: the most remarkable are ...

The place in which the unfortunate king Charles I was confined (1647), and his children imprisoned after his death: but the apartments are so dilapidated that it is next to impossible to decide upon their arrangement: the window however is shown through which he vainly attempted an escape: this is generally examined with a greater share of interest than perhaps any other part of the castle, and is often obliged to contribute as a relic, some minute portion of its crumbling walls.

THE KEEP is certainly the most ancient part of the fortress, having been built either prior to, or early in the time of the Saxons: and was rendered an appendage to the more ample fortifications constructed by the Normans. It is reached by a flight of 72 stone steps (nine inches each); was guarded by a portcullis-gate; and provided with a well 310 feet deep, since partially filled by the falling ruins.

At the S.E. angle are the remains of another very ancient tower called MONTJOY'S: the walls in some places are eighteen feet thick.

The WELL-HOUSE is to many persons the most attractive object within the walls of the castle,—for should the solemn ruins fail to impress that sentiment of reflection which proves to others the very zest of their visit, they will at least be not a little amused by the apt performance of a docile ass, whose task it is to draw up water from a well 300 feet deep! This office he performs by treading rapidly inside

20

of an immense windlass-wheel (15½ feet in diameter,) whereby he gives it the necessary rotatory motion. The natural longevity of these patient laborers is here exemplified by the instances on record; one done the duty for above 50 years, another 40, and another nearly 30. To afford some idea of the depth of the well, a lighted candle is lowered: and water is thrown down from a bucket, which produces quite a startling noise,—it will be three or four seconds in falling. For the same purpose, pins were formerly employed, but these were strictly forbidden, on account of their deleterious tendency on the water.

The Chapel, the Governor's apartments, the Barracks, Powder Magazine, &c. are also pointed out; but to go over the whole works of this venerable monument of antiquity, and give a minute detail of the several parts usually shown to strangers, would be tedious to the *reader*, though doubtless every spot and fragment must be viewed by the *visitor* with a lively interest.

If a party be not pressed for time, they should go round the outer terrace, reckoned a mile in circumference, the walk is in some parts sequestered and most pleasingly solemn, in other points presenting very charming views; and altogether calculated to raise our admiration, and give a more perfect idea of this beautiful specimen of ancient fortification.

The open space in the outworks, called the Place of Arms, is where the Archery Club resort during the season for exercise; no spot certainly could be more convenient: though by the bye, there is a degree of modish gaiety on such occasions, which is not altogether in character (at least to a picturesque eye,) with the solemnity of a scene betraying ...

"The grey and grief-worn aspect of old days!"

The military establishment of the castle is at present altogether a sinecure; formerly this was the regular seat of the insular government; but now it is quite deserted, save by the individual who has the privilege of showing the place to strangers, and his attendants.

---

## THE VILLAGE OF CARISBROOKE

Is an extremely pretty place, and still very populous, though much less so than formerly, when it enjoyed the consequence of a CITY, guarded by the only fortress in the island to which the inhabitants could fly for refuge in the moment of invasion: it rises on a hill opposite that on which stand the venerable ruins of the Castle: and in the intervening valley a beautiful stream winds its course towards Newport, sufficiently copious to turn several mills—the springs supplying water highly esteemed for its purity. The church is of great antiquity: and its tower is a very handsome specimen of Gothic architecture, proudly relieving itself from the surrounding trees and habitations. There are several genteel residences, and a few good lodging-houses in the village, whose neatly dressed gardens, interspersed with lofty trees, and environed by the most agreeable scenery, give to the place altogether an uncommon air of rural beauty.

> "How picturesque the view, where up the side
> Of that steep hill, the roofs of russet thatch
> Rise mix'd with trees, above whose swelling tops
> Ascends the tall church-tower, and loftier still
> The hill's extended ridge, crown'd with yellow corn—
> While slow beneath the bank, the silver stream
> Glides by the flowery isles and willow groves."

## NEWPORT.

*To form an idea merely of the Town, it will be sufficient for a stranger to pace two or three of the principal streets—the High-st. of course from one end to the other; he will then see the* TOWN-HALL: *the old* PARISH-CHURCH, *situated in the Corn-market; the public* LIBRARY *in the Beast-market; and the ancient* GRAMMAR-SCHOOL. *The most inviting short walks are over* MONTJOY'S *to Carisbrooke—to the top of* PAN DOWN—*and to Hurststake, on the banks of the* RIVER, *at high tide.*

NEWPORT is allowed by most travellers to be as clean and pretty a country-town as any in the kingdom. The houses are of a modern and respectable construction: the streets regular and well paved, with sufficient descent to be always clean; and two copious streams water it on the east and west.

Being closely surrounded by an amphitheatre of lofty downs, beautifully chequered by pasture and cultivation, cottages and villas,—the environs are of the most agreeable and inviting character, and the climate mild and salubrious; to those therefore who love to blend social intercourse with the pleasures of a cheerful yet quiet retreat, Newport presents many decided attractions. Years ago it was observed, that "there were few provincial towns which could afford independence more sources of rational enjoyment:" and since then there has been a great accession to the local means of intellectual pleasure, in respect of philosophical and literary institutions, private and professional reading societies, a Mechanics' Institution, circulating libraries, &c. &c. The places of public worship too have equally increased; being three episcopal (two of recent erection), two for Independents, two for Wesleyan and Primitive Methodists, a Bible-Christian, a Roman-catholic, a Unitarian, and a Particular-baptist. There are five respectable inns, in the town (see the List), and two assembly-rooms.

From its central position, it is well calculated for being the principal market-town, and, as it were the metropolis, of the island. On the Saturdays in particular, it presents a very animated scene: being frequented by all classes who are obliged to attend for the purposes of business, or upon judicial affairs; which would naturally induce many other parties to visit in favorable weather, were it only for the sake of a pleasant jaunt.

These advantages of course give it a steady trade in almost every branch of business; and latterly the shops have exchanged much of their antiquated country appearance for the more imposing style of the fashionable towns,—where dazzling glare is resorted to as the chief attraction.

Though Newport does not depend, like the watering-places, upon the annual influx of visitors engaging their lodgings for a season, yet many of the best situated and most convenient houses are handsomely fitted-up for the purpose; and should the river be ever sufficiently deepened to admit a passage steamer to ply at regular hours without regard to the state of the tide, Newport might defy all competition, by the rapid improvement of its various local capabilities which would necessarily follow.

The River (called the Medina, from dividing the island in the middle,) is navigable from Newport to Cowes for vessels of sixty or seventy tons burthen, during high water. The banks are beautifully dressed with scattered groves and copse-wood: and interspersed with the arable fields and meadows are several churches, seats, villas, farms, and cottages, on either side: and as the lands rise rather boldly, the while scene is viewed to advantage from the water, and will be found to afford a very delightful trip on a summer's day, to or from Cowes; the party leaving by the returning tide after about two hours' stay at either place.

The gayest season at Newport is during the Whitsuntide Fair, and three successive Saturdays at Michaelmas, the time when the agricultural servants receive their wages, and re-engage for the following year. The old custom of the female-servants assembling at one part of the town, and the men at another, for the purpose of engaging in new situations, is still partially kept up; these occasions are familiarly called the "Bargain-fair Saturdays," the middle or principal one falling on the first Saturday in October.

## PUBLIC BUILDINGS.

Of these the most conspicuous is the GUILDHALL, situated nearly in the centre of the town: it is rather a stately edifice of the Ionic order. Here the magistrates of the whole island meet every Saturday for hearing and deciding upon petty causes: and examining and committing prisoners to the Winchester assizes, or in, minor offences to take their trials at the quarter sessions for the Isle of Wight, formerly held at Winchester, but which are *now* very properly *adjourned*, to save the inhabitants the great inconvenience and expense of crossing the water. There are also the quarter sessions for the borough; and that excellent institution, the County Court for the settlement of small debts.—In the area beneath the hall is held the Saturday's market for poultry, eggs, and butter.

Another showy building is the ISLE OF WIGHT INSTITUTION, or permanent public Library, to which nearly all the neighbouring gentry subscribe. Besides the reading-room and library it contains a museum for local curiosities, &c. Temporary residents in the island may become subscribers for six months by a payment of 25s.

The FREE-GRAMMAR SCHOOL is the only building claiming respect for its antiquity (besides the parish-church), situated in the street leading to the Cowes road: it was erected by subscription in the year 1619, and duly endowed. Though recently having been repaired throughout, its appearance is still rather picturesque: and possesses considerable historic interest, from the memorable conference held here between the parliamentary commissioners and king Charles the

First, up to the unfortunate moment when he was unexpectedly seized and imprisoned in Hurst Castle.

The PARISH-CHURCH is considered to be of the age of Henry II, as it is dedicated to St. Thomas-a-Becket: it is spacious, and has a fine lofty square tower; but there is nothing very particular either in its architecture or antiquities to call for minute description. The chief curiosities are ... the Pulpit, remarkable for its rich and ingenious carving: a monument to Sir Edward Horsey; and the spot where the second daughter of King Charles was buried: she died while the family were prisoners at Carisbrooke—and it was only by accident in the year 1793 that the vault was discovered.—St. John's Church, built a few years ago on the south side of the town, at the foot of Montjoy's, is a conspicuous object in most points of view: and though plain in appearance, is very convenient in its interior arrangements: it is supported on the voluntary principle.

Newport returns two members to parliament.—The number of inhabitants in the town, which has considerably extended beyond the limits of the borough, is about 7000. The corporate body consists of 24 members; but since the passing of the Municipal Reform Act, there can of course be nothing peculiar in their constitution of which the reader need be informed.

A Lace-factory on a very extensive scale is established just without the town, on the east side, going to Ryde: in the town is also an establishment which gives employment to many females in the lace-embroidering process.

*The Environs of Newport.*

The following villages and hamlets are nearly connected with, or gradually approximating the town:—

On the eastern side, surrounded by meadows, is BARTON's VILLAGE, near which a neat little church has lately been opened, on the road to Ryde;—just above it is a gentleman's seat called BELLECROFT.

SHIDE, half a mile to the south, is picturesquely seated at the foot of the steep and high down called Pan: the river Medina flows through the grounds, and there are several respectable villas in its immediate neighbourhood.

Westward is the NEW VILLAGE, a street of genteel and comfortable houses (some of which are furnished for lodgings,) leading to Carisbrooke: behind it is the hill called Montjoy's, from whose lofty summit is obtained the most comprehensive view of Newport, its river, and the adjacent country. There is also a small hamlet on HUNNY-HILL, north of the town.

FAIRLEE is a principal seat, a mile north of Newport. The house is large and of respectable appearance: standing at the head of an extensive and beautiful lawn which slopes to the eastern bank of the river, surrounded by close and open groves.

About a mile from Newport, on the road to West Cowes, stands the HOUSE OF INDUSTRY, a very large building, generally containing between 500 and 600 paupers; it includes within its walls a lunatic asylum, hospital, school, and chapel: and has an extensive garden attached.

Its internal affairs and out-door relief are regulated by a Board of Guardians and Directors, consisting of a certain number of respectable inhabitants, chosen from every parish in the island,— under the provisions of an Act of Parliament obtained in the year 1770 for the parochial consolidation of the whole island. They are therefore independent of the Poor-law Commissioners, and have adopted only as much as they thought proper of the general statute.

ALBANY BARRACKS, on the opposite side of the road, are capable of accommodating nearly 2000 troops—for a long time however the complement stationed here seldom exceeded a few companies, and for months together there would not be even a serjeant's guard: but latterly the depots of several regiments have been removed hither: so that there are now often from 1000 to 1500 men at the same time.

Westward of the Barracks, bordering the Yarmouth road, is the extensive tract called PARKHURST FOREST, planted a few years since with oaks and Scotch firs, by order of Government.

PARKHURST PRISON, to the north of the barracks, is an extensive range of buildings, dedicated to the benevolent purpose of reclaiming from infamy, if possible, a large number of juvenile criminals of the male sex.

To accomplish this truly desirable object (as *punishment* ought certainly to be *corrective* in the best sense of the word), the boys are regularly instructed by competent tradesmen, in such branches of popular business as may be best suited to their respective capacities: in conjunction with the most approved course of common school-education. Particular attention is likewise paid to the elevation of their moral character, so likely to be permanently influenced by means of impressive friendly admonition, the frequent inculcation and daily observance of religious duties, and the exciting hope of reward for good behaviour in a mitigation of their sentence: in short, by the most encouraging and kind treatment, as far as is compatible with the strictness of prison discipline. None therefore, but the thoroughly incorrigible, can leave the institution without being greatly improved in their habits and dispositions, if not altogether reformed; since *Order, Cleanliness, Activity,* and *Industry,* must become almost natural to them by the time they are discharged,—their understandings cultivated, and their minds more or less impressed with the sentiments of virtue and religion.

It would be injudicious to enter in detail on the subject of the routine management, or the particular discipline adopted in the respective wards: as very probably many alterations will be introduced from time to time, as experiment and practice may suggest: and moreover, as a "Report" is annually published by order of Government (at a low price), containing the most minute particulars in every department of the Asylum. For the same reasons we have avoided any description of the architectural plan of the prison, a pretty good idea of which may be formed in passing by on the high-road.—We must however mention one fact that speaks highly favorably of the salutary system adopted, namely, that during the five years from the opening of the institution in 1838, there occurred but two deaths among the boys, though the number averaged about 250 at the same time.

The establishment has been visited by several eminent persons, who, after having particularly examined the course adopted in every department, expressed themselves so well pleased with its management and beneficial tendency, that another building at a short distance was erected in 1843; and altogether there is sufficient room now for 700 or 800 delinquents. No stranger is admitted without an order from the Home Secretary of State.

The newly erected residences of the officers and other parties connected with the prison, barracks, &c., altogether form quite a village, known by the general term of Parkhurst.

## WEST COWES.

☞ *The transient visitor here should immediately inquire for the* PARADE—*pass by the* CASTLE *on the beach, to the bathing-machines— retrograde by the carriage-road under the* NEW CHURCH—*mount the hill at the back of the Castle—reach the* OLD CHURCH, *which is contiguous to* NORTHWOOD PARK—*and then return, to cross over to E. Cowes.*

The decided advantages of Cowes are ... its excellent shore for bathing—and its safe and commodious harbour—which recommend it strongly as a fashionable watering-place, and the resort of gentlemen fond of aquatic amusements.

The appearance of this town from the water, particularly when approached by the passage from Southampton, is extremely pleasing; as the acclivity of the hill on which it stands is sufficiently bold to admit of the houses being seen above each other, as if built on a succession of terraces, while their starting formality is charmingly relieved by the intervening shrubberies and groups of lofty trees. To a stranger however, who may confine his walk to the streets just where he lands, this favorable impression would be almost obliterated,—for they are both narrow and crowded: though in these respects there is some improvement the further he goes either to the east or the west; but it is near the Castle that he must look for the greatest share of united beauty and respectability. The truth is, the lower part near the quay is of course occupied by tradesmen, for the advantages of business, and convenient landing-places; and as their houses stand at the edge of the water, many parties prefer their lodgings to those in the more open quarters on the top of the hill,—and many of them are therefore elegantly furnished for letting.

THE PARADE affords a delightful promenade, being on the water's edge. Here are several first-rate houses, standing at the foot of the steepest part of the hill, which is luxuriantly clothed with hanging shrubberies and several groups of majestic trees, presenting a perfectly unique picture of sylvan and marine beauty. The Royal Yacht-Club House, with its ample awning, and the very elegant Gothic villa of Sir John Hippesley, will be particularly noticed.

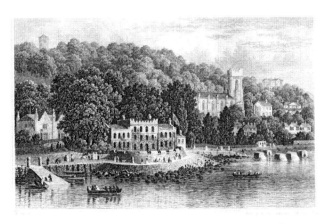

## THE CASTLE, WEST COWES, ISLE OF WIGHT

THE CASTLE stands westward of the Parade: but were it not for a small battery of eleven guns in front, the stranger might search in vain for a fabric which he could identify as "a Castle," at least by any portion of its modernized architecture and surrounding embellishments. In fact, the original dwelling was a few years ago greatly enlarged—made a story higher—the open ground at the back inclosed (!)—with other alterations to render it a fit residence for nobility. It was built by king Henry VIII, about the same time as those at Sandown, Yarmouth, and Calshot, for the purpose of securing the coast against the then frequent attacks of pirates, as well as the more formidable invasions of the French.

Beyond the Castle are the bathing-machines; the villas of Earl Belfast and Lord Grantham; and behind these several others built in various tasty styles, and acquiring a picturesque effect from being more or less screened by the copse-wood on the steep slope at their back. But the chief ornament of this quarter is the new Episcopal chapel, whether viewed near, or from a distance on the water,—being a chastely-elegant structure in the Gothic style, in a most commanding situation: it is private property. Should the stranger feel disposed to extend his walk for about a mile further on the beach, which he would find very agreeable—he will come to a gentleman's residence distinguished by an air of antiquity, named Westcliff, though the neighbourhood is popularly called EGYPT.

We make this remark, because there is a lane close by, which turns up to the high-road from Cowes to Gurnard Bay, and by this road we would recommend the visitor by all means to return, for the sake of the magnificent prospect which it affords, and on the peculiar character of which the *permanent* attractions of the place so much depend. But to do this justice, the reader must have recourse to his Map. The most prominent objects are Calshot Castle, standing apparently isolated at the mouth of Southampton Water, and the tall tower of Eaglehurst, seated on the neighbouring shore.

By "permanent attractions," we mean, that many landscapes of the most romantic character fail to attract our attention for any considerable time, on *repeated* visits, if destitute of those ever-varying circumstances which have in some degree the interest of NOVELTY such for instance as the rural, and more particularly the *marine* prospects of the Isle of Wight; these afford an endless source of amusement to the speculative eye, — whether directed to the soft and gradual changes on the variegated face of Nature *under cultivation,* or to the more animated, and constantly shifting scene exhibited in a crowded sea-port, or where there are other safe and ample roadsteds for the heaviest ships of war. In these advantages Cowes and Ryde stand pre-eminent.

> "Scenes must he beautiful, which daily viewed,
> Please daily, and whose novelty survives
> Long knowledge, and the scrutiny of years —
> Praise justly due to those that I describe"

We are now supposed to have reached the top of the hill, where the old CHURCH is situated: this is a spacious, plain building, having a very tall square tower, as destitute of beauty as anything of the kind can well be: yet as it peers loftily above all the surrounding objects, is a great improvement to the outline of the hill, when viewed from any considerable distance. Contiguous to the crowded cemetery stands ...

NORTHWOOD HOUSE, a large and elegant mansion in the Palladian style of architecture. The PARK is an extensive demesne, and profusely planted; there are however comparatively few of those venerable sylvan honors which constitute the beauty of park-scenery.

On the eastern slope of the hill, where the high-road turns off for Newport, stands WESTHILL, a charming cottage-ornee in the centre of a smooth sloping lawn interspersed with magnificent elms and close shrubberies.—In the environs of Cowes are several other genteel residences: MOOR-HOUSE is distinguished by its Gothic pinnacles and commanding station: and near Gurnard Bay is a pretty retired seat, appropriately called WOOD-VALE.

Besides the two churches, there are Catholic, Independent, and Wesleyan chapels. There are three large Hotels (see the List), and several minor places of good accommodation; reading-rooms, a Mechanics' Institution, &c.

## EAST COWES.

☞ *The town itself has nothing to interest a stranger: but in the vicinity are several first-rate seats and marine villas—the most distinguished being* OSBORNE, NORRIS, *and* EAST COWES CASTLE.

This little town is separated from West Cowes by the river Medina, which here joins the sea. From the unexpected concurrence of various favorable circumstances, it is looking-up to be a place of some importance: the value of property has already considerably advanced, and trade in general improved. It has one good Hotel, several respectable lodging-houses: a neat episcopalian church, and an Independent chapel. Having a large shipwright's yard, and a number of marine stores, wharfs, &c., where merchant-ships lie alongside to take in or unload their cargoes, it often exhibits much of the bustling appearance of a sea-port town. There is a private landing-place near the ferry, for the accommodation of Her Majesty. The Custom-house has been removed to the other side of the harbour.

The immediate neighbourhood of East Cowes has long been extremely beautiful, from being almost entirely covered with charming seats and villas, whose luxuriant groves and shrubberies give the scenery an uncommonly rich effect: and her Majesty having made this part of the island her marine residence, it now possesses a proud distinction in point of interest with the British public.

A stranger should make his perambulation by first ascending the hill by the *old* carriage-road, passing several villas (see list) secluded by dense shrubberies and large trees; a circumstance little to be regretted, as their chief boast is the amenity of their location. But through the tall plantations on the right our eye will be delightfully attracted by the picturesque turrets of East Cowes Castle, and the surrounding beautiful grounds. At the pretty lodge-entrance to the castle, the road divides, — the left-hand branch running to Norris, the right to Osborne and Newport; and in about eight or ten minutes' further walk, we can return by the new road through "East Cowes Park."

OSBORNE, ISLE OF WIGHT

*The Principal Seats near East Cowes.*

OSBORNE, the property of HER MOST GRACIOUS MAJESTY, is entitled, equally from public interest and its own importance, to the first notice under this head.—The situation is everyway eligible for the *marine* residence of a sovereign of the British Isles: for it commands a most extensive and *animated* prospect, including Spithead and other naval stations: has a beautiful sea-beach (with a private landing-place); and is sheltered by extensive woods and plantations. The original seat was a plain family mansion surrounded by park-like grounds, which have been extended by the purchase of several farms—including BARTON (whose fine old Elizabethan manor-house has received a complete and judicious reparation): so that the estate is now most conveniently bounded on the west by the high-road from East Cowes to Newport; on the south by a branch of the same road to Ryde; on the east by a sheltered cove called King's Quay (as tradition will have it from the circumstance of King John there concealing himself for a time when opposed by the barons): and on the north-east by the beautiful Solent Channel. Thus compassed by the sea and the best roads in the island, it extends from north to south about two miles and a half, by nearly two miles from east to west; enjoying the most delightful variety of scenery, from the simple picture of rural life to the grandeur of our NAVAL GLORY, and the majesty of the ocean itself.

The quality of the soil differs very considerably; but the worst is well adapted for oak-plantations; and the thorough draining and other improvements now carrying on will make the whole admirably suited for agricultural pursuits, to which H.R.H. the Prince Consort is very partial. A great part of the estate is enclosed by a park-fence; and through the luxuriant woods and undulating grounds, several miles of excellent private carriage-roads have been constructed, much more being in progress.

The PALACE occupies the site of the old house; it is in the Palladian style (which so admirably admits the application to domestic architecture of the most beautiful features of the Grecian orders).

Within the ballustrade of its lofty flat roof is a charming promenade in fine weather.

The flag-tower is 107 feet in height, the clock-tower 90, the first terrace-wall 17, and the second 10. The Royal Apartments are contained in the loftiest part of the building—they are handsome and spacious, and standing altogether in advance, command on every side the most uninterrupted views: at the back is the flag-tower, communicating with an open corridor which extends the whole of the north-west face of the building; and on the other side of the tower is the carriage-entrance, opening on pleasure-grounds adorned with the choicest varieties of ornamental shrubs—thriving with a luxuriance which promises well for the appearance of the estate, when the whole shall have been finished. The builder is T. Cubitt, esq.; but the design, we believe, was principally furnished by His Royal Highness Prince Albert himself—whose taste, and knowledge of the fine arts, well qualify him for the undertaking.

As it would be almost impossible to convey by verbal description a correct idea of the general appearance of this noble structure, we beg to refer our readers to the annexed Engraving—and also to the Views of Osborne, recently published in the "Vectis Scenery," and which may be purchased separately at 1s. each.

NORRIS is a noble specimen of the castellated mansion, having been built in imitation of an ancient Norman fabric—massive in its construction, and remarkable for a stern simplicity of style disdaining all minute decoration. From this circumstance, and some of the loftiest towers being enveloped in the most luxuriant ivy, the whole building has so venerable an air of antiquity, even when closely examined, that we can hardly suppose it to be the production of modern days: and enjoying too as it does an uncommonly fine position on the most northern hill of the island, its general aspect is truly magnificent in every point of view. It is scarcely necessary to add, that the castle commands a most interesting marine prospect.

Some of the rooms are of elegant dimensions, and the arrangement of the whole considered good—such indeed might be expected from the reputation of the architect, the late Mr. Wyatt. The stables, &c., are also on a very ample scale, and in the same plain, substantial style as the castle, for which they have not unfrequently been taken by strangers at the first glance.

The grounds are now well timbered: the plantations beautifully dressing the steep slope even to the water's edge. The utmost privacy might be enjoyed, for there is the accommodation of a good landing-place, and a carriage-road thence to the house.

Norris was the property of the late Lord Henry Seymour, who was engaged many years in its construction, and must in the course of a long period have expended immense sums in improvements that may be said to be now buried from our view. After his demise, it was two seasons chosen for the residence of their R.H. the Duchess of Kent and the Princess Victoria (during which time the latter improved remarkably in her health): and has since been purchased on very moderate terms by R. Bell, esq.—who greatly extended the scope of the grounds by fresh purchases of land, especially by some belonging to the Osborne estate—previously to her Majesty's negociating for its possession.

EAST COWES CASTLE, which enjoys a truly enviable site (for it combines an uncommon degree of shelter with the most extensive and *animated* prospect), is built in the bold style usually termed the Moorish, and has three handsome fronts of varied elevations, with a tasteful diversity of towers, mantled more or less by the most luxuriant ivy, and a great variety of elegant flowering plants. The Conservatory is a splendid addition; and the grounds, though not extensive, are very beautiful.

East Cowes Castle was built by, and continued for many years to be the favorite residence of the late John Nash, esq., and was with him a sort of architectural pet, receiving from time to time such additions and alterations as appeared to be improvements to the general design, or called for on the score of enlarged accommodation; a circumstance certainly not calculated to insure the greatest amount of domestic convenience (as regards the size and arrangement of the rooms), though no doubt contributing largely to the picturesque effect of the exterior. On Mr. Nash's demise it was purchased by Earl Shannon,—and after his death by N. Barwell, esq., who in 1846 sold off all the furniture, and valuable productions of art which adorned this beautiful object of interest to visitors.

## "EAST COWES PARK"

Is the title of a very extensive building speculation, which comprehends above 100 acres of land, lying between Osborne and East Cowes. This tract was a few years back laid out for the erection of a number of elegant villa-residences, each to be surrounded with its garden and shrubbery, yet to command a delightful marine view. Excellent roads were made, having on either side a foot-path, flower-border, and neat iron pallisade; handsome gateways erected; and a pier, botanic garden, and other attractive improvements commenced or projected. The speculation did not however meet the success it merited, and comparatively few houses have as yet been built.

## THE HARBOUR,

To which Cowes is principally indebted for its origin and present importance, enjoys a high character for safety as well as convenience: it is used by vessels of heavy tonnage, either in waiting for a favorable wind, or for the purpose of repairing damages sustained at sea; and after stormy weather, is often crowded with ships of various nations, in addition to those registered at the place—this being the port for the whole island.

There are spacious dockyards, patent slips, &c., both at East and West Cowes: at the latter, excellent dry docks. The naval builders have long held a high reputation for skill: several men-of-war were built here during the last century; and of late years numerous beautiful pleasure-yachts, merchantmen, sloops of war, and other vessels—including the *Medina*, a first-rate steam-ship (lost on the West India passage), and some large steamers for various foreign governments.

## THE ROYAL-YACHT-SQUADRON

Make Cowes their port of rendezvous: they contribute largely to the maritime gaiety of the place, and give particular classes of tradesmen an extensive share of employment; but the town altogether does not, it is said, derive that degree of fostering patronage from their presence which might be expected. The *Royal Thames Yacht-club* often make this their summer-station.

## THE REGATTA

Generally takes place in August, and is an exciting source of hilarity with the inhabitants of Cowes, as well as numerous visitors from every part of the island and opposite coast,—should the weather prove favorable at the time. The sailing-matches are now mostly confined to the members of the Royal Yacht-squadrons: and it is to be regretted, that owing to the distance which they sail, and the number of days engaged, comparatively little pleasure is afforded to the mere spectator: there is however usually one day's continued amusement—when sailing and rowing matches for liberal subscription-prizes likewise take place between the local watermen, &c.—excellent bands of music attend,—and in the evening there is a brilliant display of fire-works, both from the shore and from the yachts in various parts of the harbour. On these occasions the appearance of the whole is animated beyond description; and to a person from the country, the exhibition of such a numerous assemblage of the most beautiful vessels in the world must prove a lively gratification, for they are of every size and variety of rig, from the stately ship of 4 or 500 tons burthen down to the yawl of only 10.

Cowes lies extremely convenient for parties fond of aquatic trips: for which purpose a number of experienced watermen ply excellent boats: they are most frequently engaged in the short and pleasant excursions to Beaulieu, Netley, Southampton (on the opposite coast), and Newport; sometimes to Alum Bay, and even for a voyage round the island.

The bathing here is considered very excellent: particularly so at W. Cowes, from the boldness and pebbly character of the beach, admitting the machines to be put in requisition in all states of the tide,—a very great advantage. There are also hot and other baths for the use of invalids, both at the machines and at certain parts of the town.

*The Road from East Cowes to Ryde.*

WHIPPINGHAM CHURCH stands near the second mile-stone, on the ascent of a hill rising from the eastern bank of the Medina: it is perhaps the neatest *old* ecclesiastical structure in the island, and is frequently attended by her Majesty and Prince Albert when residing at Osborne. Close by are the Parsonages and PADMORE HOUSE, embosomed in groves, and commanding an extensive prospect—the nearest object on the opposite side of the river being the ancient though plain church of Northwood. Altogether this is a very pleasing rural spot, and to visit it will make the difference of only a few minutes in diverging from the regular road.

## WOOTTON-BRIDGE.

Here we pass over an inlet of the sea, indifferently called Fishbourne Creek or Wootton River; the cottages border the road on either side, and have a remarkably clean and comfortable appearance. There are also a few good houses: the Parsonage, though rather secluded, enjoys a charming marine prospect; and *Kite-hill* will be known by its antique aspect and screen of lofty firs. But the pride of the place is FERNHILL, a first-rate seat: the house is built in the light Gothic style, and stands at the head of an extensive lawn sloping to the water, interspersed with groups of trees and flourishing plantations.

We shall often see the prospect-tower of Fernhill peering above the masses of variegated foliage; and indeed the whole has much the air of a religious structure, enjoying one of those happy localities which distinguished such retreats of former days. The opposite banks of the river, or rather lake, are clothed with the finest oak-woods in the island, feathering from the very water's edge; and the whole neighbourhood presents the rich appearance of an extensive forest covering hill and dale. Should therefore the visitor reach this spot at the favorable concurrence of high water on a calm sunny day, he will agree with us that the whole forms a splendid landscape, — *rock* being in fact the only feature denied to make it perfect.

Excellent roads have recently been made (by the proprietor of the estate,) on the west side of the river, below the bridge: affording a very pleasant drive; and as they open many delightful sites, will probably cause a considerable accession of buildings in that direction.

At the mouth of the creek on the east side is a large hamlet called FISHHOUSE, including a dockyard, where several frigates have been built.

WOOTTON COMMON is a mile nearer Newport: and affords an instance within a few years of a wild tract of gorse and brambles being profitably converted to tillage and garden. Here too are several scattered dwellings forming an improving hamlet; and in one of them (called in courtesy *Landscape Cottage,*) was produced *in all its stages* the present little work, as well as its other kindred publications.

About midway between Wootton and Ryde, on the sea side of the road, we pass the remains of

## QUARR ABBEY,

The most considerable ecclesiastical establishment ever founded in the Isle of Wight, which had, like every other part of Great Britain, previous to the Reformation, its full share of monastic and other religious institutions. This was among the first settlements of the Cistercian Order in England, having been built in the 12th century; was most amply endowed, and had several illustrious persons buried in the chapel, to whose memory sumptuous monuments were erected; but after its dissolution, the property was purchased by a merchant of Southampton, and the sacred edifice *reduced for the value of the bare materials.*

The merchant's son afterwards sold the estate to the Lord Chief Justice, Sir Thomas Fleming, with whose descendants it still remains. Some of the outer walls are still extant, and must have circumscribed at least 20 acres. A foot-path passes through the grounds to Ryde, &c.

Of this once-magnificent establishment little now remains; merely portions of the appendant offices, which were converted into barns, &c., for farm-purposes. What was spared in the moment of ruthless spoliation, lay long buried under heaps of rubbish and weeds—till a few years since, when one of the occupiers, with laudable zeal, rescued from total annihilation the few remaining fragments, which are now open to the view of strangers.

## The other Religious Structures

Scattered through the island were ... a Priory at St. Helen's; one at Appuldurcombe; one at St. Cross, near Newport; and another at Carisbrooke, vestiges of which may still be traced; together with a great number of oratories, chantries, chapels, and religious houses, amounting in the whole to 70 or 80, exclusive of the regular parish-churches;—and yet scarcely any of these interesting monuments have survived their reckless doom to ruin and neglect; not even a spiry fragment sufficiently large or romantic to form a pleasing subject for the pencil, invite the mind to contemplation, or aid the poet's retrospective muse.

BINSTEAD, to which there is a good foot-path from Quarr through the woods, is about a mile westward of Ryde. Several genteel residences, mostly built in a pleasing cottage-style, adorned by groups of trees and shrubs, are scattered over a wide space of broken ground, where extensive stone-quarries have been worked for many centuries. It is a favorite walk with the inhabitants of Ryde, across the fields to the church (not seen from the road), which has lately been considerably enlarged and improved. The names of the respective villas will be found in the List of Seats.

## RYDE.

☞ *The best may of seeing this populous town, by those who have little inclination, or perhaps less time, for perambulation is, from the Pier, to enquire first for* BRIGSTOCK TERRACE*—walk on for about five minutes still westward—returning, pass by the* CHURCH, *and round the* TOWN-HALL, *and Market-place,* ST. JAMES'S CHAPEL, *and the Theatre;—look into the* ARCADE, *a little below;—traverse the street nearly opposite the theatre,*

*which will open the eastern part of the town, where there is a handsome*
NEW CHURCH—*and the very agreeable Environs in the direction of Appley*
*and St. John's, which ought to be visited if time could be spared, going first*
*on the beach, and returning by the high-road, a circuit of about two miles.*

RYDE, ISLE OF WIGHT.

Ryde now ranks the first town in the island for the number of its elegant *modern* erections, both public and private; and if building should be carried on with an equal degree of spirit for a few years more, it will also be considerably the most populous. It occupies two sides of a lofty hill, falling with a regular descent to the sea on the north, opposite Portsmouth, from which it is about five miles across. This short passage, from its perfect safety and general convenience, proves a great local advantage, being performed several times a-day by superior steam-vessels in about half an hour. But besides these established means of conveyance, large-sized wherries (most excellent sea-boats,) are in constant attendance to take parties across on moderate terms, or for hire by the day upon any aquatic trip, even to Brighton.

The town used formerly to be distinguished into Upper and Lower Ryde, from having several fields between, but now it is only the difference of position which calls for any term of distinction; for where the green meadows then formed the separation, is now the most closely built upon; and at the beginning of this century, Yelf's Hotel stood a new and isolated object.

The principal streets are very open, clean, and well-paved; regularly disposed, most of them crossing each other nearly at right angles. Several of the handsomest run parallel almost in a direct line to the beach, thus affording the very desirable advantage of an interesting sea-view.

THE PIER being the first object to interest a stranger, and having contributed more than anything else to the advancement of the town, is well entitled to priority of notice.

Up to the year 1814, when it was constructed by a company in subscription shares of £.50 each, landing or embarking was rendered generally a miserable task, except during very favorable weather, at the moment of high tide. The practice then was, to cram the passengers promiscuously into a common luggage-cart, till it was drawn out upon the almost level sands sufficiently far for a large wherry to float alongside, into which they were then transferred, and conveyed to the sailing-packet, perhaps lying off at some considerable distance. The reader will readily believe that this united cart and boat process of reaching the vessel or shore could not be very inviting at the best of times; but it was really terrific to weak and timid persons during the concurrence of a heavy rain, and the tide perhaps at its lowest ebb!—to say nothing of the horrors of a dark and squally night.

The length of the Pier is now nearly half a mile (being double the extent it was originally), having had 500 feet added in the year 1824: the same augmentation again in 1833; and in 1842 it received the crowning addition of a most spacious and well constructed HEAD, which was rendered everyway more convenient for passengers landing or embarking. This last improvement must afford a most delightful accommodation for the gentry who prefer the pier for their usual promenade; and where, from the great extent it stretches out into the open sea, those invalids who are precluded from exercise, may more conveniently enjoy the invigorating sea-breeze. It is firmly constructed of timber: has four or five landing-places at different distances to suit the state of the tide: a strong railing on each side; and is furnished with several open and covered seats.

## PRINCIPAL BUILDINGS.

The TOWN-HALL and MARKET-HOUSE affords the best proof of the public spirit of the inhabitants of Hyde in regard to local improvements: for this handsome edifice is on a scale to accommodate three or four times the present population. It was first opened in the year 1831: and the commissioners for improving the town endeavoured to establish a permanent market for cattle, &c., to be held in the large open space in front, but the attempt proved abortive—Newport lying so much more conveniently for the general resort of agriculturists and tradesmen from every quarter of the island.—It is remarkable, however, considering the spirit of the inhabitants for public improvements, that it should have been left to the year 1840, before the town was lighted with gas!

The ARCADE is an elegant piece of architecture, though it does not make that imposing figure of its exterior, which the visitor would expect, when previously told that it cost at least £10,000. It contains 14 shops, and a very large room for the exhibition and sale of works of art: every portion being finished in the best style of workmanship.

This bold undertaking for a private individual, we are sorry to say, has not yet realized a remunerating return. The mistake seems to have been in fixing upon a site which had no local advantages to recommend it for a fashionable promenade; nor likely ever to become a much-frequented thoroughfare, popular and busy. Moreover, the tradesmen generally find it more to their advantage to engage respectable houses in the best streets, where they can profitably let lodgings, and make a much more attractive exhibition of their goods. These remarks will also serve to explain, why comparatively so few persons avail themselves of the extensive accommodation which the Market-house affords.

BRIGSTOCK TERRACE is a fine range of first-rate houses built according to a very judicious, uniform design, furnished by the late Mr. J. Sanderson. They command a beautiful marine prospect, as they stand at the head of a sloping lawn-like field, interspersed with several oaks and elms: indeed the terrace is the most conspicuous part of Ryde when viewed from the sea.

On the west side of the town too is a very spacious square, comprising a great variety of tastefully-embellished mansions; indeed in every direction a number of elegant houses are constructing,—tenants being found for most of them even before they are completed.

A very few years ago it was quite an easy task to point out by distinctive marks all the most important houses—it was only to name *Westmont,* and the two unobtrusive villas of the Duke of Buckingham and Earl Spencer. The stranger could then have no difficulty in discriminating these: but now, to give a List of all the residences that are entitled to notice with an equal share of pretensions, however judiciously described, would prove perfectly futile, and only calculated to mislead the stranger.

CHURCHES and other public places of divine worship.—These of course increase with the population; for only as late as the year 1827, the old chapel, now distinguished by its graceful spire (and seen at the back of the terrace), was so inadequate in its accommodations, as to require being considerably enlarged: and in the same year another was commenced as a private speculation by Hughes Hughes, esq., this is a long, low edifice, remarkable for its neat interior: a third has since been erected on the eastern side of the town, of a handsome design both inside and out, and very conspicuous from its open situation and lofty spire:—all three being episcopalian chapels of ease to Newchurch. The Independents, Wesleyans, and Primitive-methodists have also their respective chapels, and one for Catholic worship has been lately built, of the most elaborate style of architecture, especially the interior.

THE FAMILY HOTELS, INNS, &C.—Of these there are several, of various ranks, some of them vying in splendor and extent of accommodation with the best in the county (see the List). The lodging-houses are of course very numerous, and in every grade, from the humble *jessamy* or *myrtle* cottage at 20 or 30 shillings per week, to the lordly mansion at as many guineas.

During the latter summer months, the theatre is usually opened by a talented company of comedians. The shops are generally very imposingly fitted-up and well stocked: and in the literary and fancy lines are several excellent establishments—news-rooms, circulating-libraries, bazaars, &c.

*Aquatic Amusements, &c. at Ryde.*

THE ROYAL VICTORIA YACHT-CLUB, established in 1845, numbers amongst its members many gentlemen of the highest rank, and owners of as fine yachts as any in the world. Their Club-house is a handsome and commodious building on the beach west of the Pier; and they have an annual Regatta in the latter part of the summer, when several pieces of plate, etc., are sailed for by the vessels of this and other clubs. There is also a TOWN REGATTA held about the same time, for the purpose of giving encouragement to the skilful and deserving watermen: the sailing matches being between the wherries of the place, which are of a large size, and esteemed by nautical men to be the finest sea-boats in the kingdom: and as the race is confined to a circuit which can be distinctly seen from the whole of the Pier, there is as much interest excited as if the prizes were contested between larger craft. Rowing-matches also take place; good bands attend—and the diversions of the day usually end with a splendid display of fireworks, a dinner, or a ball. In short, nothing can exceed the gaiety of the scene, when the weather is at all fine: as it is made the occasion of a general festivity by the inhabitants—and resorted to as a holiday by great numbers from Newport, and the eastern parts of the island.

THE SHORE presents, when the tide is at its lowest ebb, a wide expanse of sand, stretching for miles both eastward and westward of the Pier, preserving upon an average the breadth of a mile: here and there interspersed with ledges of rock, and the banks beautifully feathered with groves and shrubberies. In some parts the sand has accumulated over the mud in sufficient quantity to bear wheel-carriages (which is the case near the Pier): and is found to be gradually increasing both in depth and extent. The best time to take a walk upon the shore is directly after the tide has begun to ebb,—for the sand is then firm and cool to the feet; but after a few hours' powerful sun in calm weather, it is rendered sufficiently hot to give the flowing sea almost the temperature of a warm bath, on which account the bathing here is preferred by many parties to a bolder shore.

That part called the DUVER (now built on,) was remarkable as having been chosen for interring the crew of the Royal George, a ship of 108 guns, which sank at Spithead on August 29th, 1782, by a sudden squall, while undergoing a careening of her bottom, when nearly 1000 persons perished.

Near the Pier are the bathing-machines, well attended, and in full operation; together with hot, tepid, and other baths for invalids.

THE PROSPECT.—As the *amenity* of every situation depends, we consider, greatly on the range and beauty of the view which it commands, we here give a faint sketch of the one obtained from Ryde and its neighbourhood: by which, however imperfect, it will be seen by the reader, that few prospects in England can surpass this, perhaps even in point of pleasing composition—but certainly not as *a perpetual source of the most amusing observation.*

The foreground of the Pier generally presents a most animated picture,—crowded with promenading fashionables; and surrounded by numerous wherries, steam-packets, and other craft, at anchor or gaily sailing about; a busy scene which forms a striking contrast to the quiet sylvan charms of the home-coast extending many miles east and west, and embellished by several delightful villas and other marine residences, among which are Osborne Palace (indicated by a lofty prospect-tower),—and Norris Castle, just beyond. We have the Solent Channel seen from here to peculiar advantage,—on the one hand contracting to the appearance of a noble river, and on the other expanding and uniting with the open sea. The far-famed anchorage of Spithead occupies the centre, with St. Helen's to the eastward, for ships of war; and westward, the Motherbank and Stokes's Bay, for merchantmen and colliers; hourly altering their position with the changing tides, and their number as suddenly increased or diminished with every adverse or propitious breeze.

> "Majestic o'er the sparkling tide,
>  See the tall vessel sail,
> With swelling winds, in shadowy pride,
>  A swan before the gale!"

The eye is soon caught by a splendid range of houses called Anglesea Villa, on the opposite nearest shore, contiguous to Monkton Fort; and is thence carried to immense mass of brick buildings that form the grand naval hospital of Haslar, with the town of Gosport in its rear; opposite which are the celebrated fortifications of Portsmouth, with its noble harbour affording calm security to the maritime glory of England:—Southsea Castle stands a little to the eastward, and beyond that is the low level of Hayling Island, where several handsome houses have recently been built.

The line of Portsdown hills, on one of which is Nelson's monumental pillar, usually bounds the view to the north; but in clear weather our range of perspective embraces a portion of the South Downs which is crossed by the London road near Petersfield: and on the left, the beautiful retiring banks of Southampton Water to the town to itself, backed by the woodland heights of the New Forest;—while to the right it extends to the spire of Chichester Cathedral; but with the aid of a glass even to Beachy-head, which appears in the east like a faint cloud upon the horizon of the sea.

## THE ENVIRONS OF RYDE

May be characterized as being beautifully rural, enlivened by peeps oɪ open prospects of the sea: for this is the best wooded quarter of the island, adorned with several charming seats and villas, and intersected by good roads.

But perhaps it ought to be here explained to the stranger, that by *good* roads, in the Isle of Wight, is only meant that they are kept in tolerably good order: not that they are level, or even gently undulating: for the very charm of the island consists in its sudden alternation of hill and dale, producing a constant change of scenery: one moment you may be enclosed in a sylvan theatre; and the next minute stand on the brow of a hill, sufficiently lofty to command an interminable panoramic prospect of land and sea.

We will first conduct our friends along the shore *eastward* of the town, for the distance of two or three miles. The principal objects to the westward have been already noticed (p. 41, &c.)

APPLEY (about half a mile,) is a marine villa celebrated for its amenity: hence an excellent road to St. John's, where several very eligible sites for building on are to be disposed of: and a neat little church has recently been erected.

ST. CLARE, another delightful residence: the house built in the castellated style: and the pleasure-grounds and very extensive gardens, truly exquisite.

PUCKPOOL, a sequestered Swiss Cottage.

SPRING-VALE, a pretty hamlet composed of lodging-houses.—A carriage-road hence by the back of St. Clare.

SEA-VIEW (two miles), another pleasant hamlet, containing several lodging-houses: and having near it the beautiful villas of SEA-FIELD, FAIRY-HILL, SEA-GROVE, &c. A road hence to Nettlestone Green.

The grounds of the Priory extend eastward for about a mile: the sandy beach the whole of the distance is remarkably fine.

☞ *From the above it is apparent, that a Party may have a very pleasant saunter just as far as may prove agreeable, according to their ability for walking; as there is a choice of roads by which to return, thus making a circuit of any extent they like.*

We now start by the regular carriage-road for the rocky coast (commonly called the Back of the island), and first reach a hamlet on the rise of the next hill, named OAK-FIELD, and then ...

ST. JOHN's, a first-rate seat,—mansion plain, but admirably situated for prospect, and screened by beautiful wood, as will appear in the road making several sudden turns, over-arched by lofty trees, especially the silver fir. Shortly the tower of St. Clare appears on our left: WESTRIDGE in a valley on the right; and several other minor seats are successively passed,—some partially seen through the woods and shrubberies, and others quite secluded.

☞ From the hamlet called *Nettlestone Green* (about two miles from Ryde,) a carriage-road leads down to Sea-view, by which the party may on another occasion return on the beach to Ryde, passing the back of St. Clare.

THE PRIORY is three miles from Ryde: it takes its name from having been the site of an ancient monastic cell—is a spacious, plain mansion, and ranks among the finest seats in the island: here too, much of the wood is uncommonly fine, notwithstanding its exposure to the sea-air. Arriving at ...

ST. HELEN's GREEN,

We are presented with a beautiful view of the Peninsula of Bembridge, Brading Haven, and the British Channel. The houses are mostly scattered round a large verdant square (which gives the name): and a spacious building, to answer the purposes both of a parish school and chapel, has been lately supplied by the liberality of a resident gentleman. But the chief object of curiosity here is THE OLD CHURCH-TOWER, *standing now at the water's edge*, and still struggling against the further "encroachment of the sea," which in the year 1719, was such as to oblige the parishioners to build another place of worship in a more secure situation: this we passed near the Priory. The old tower was strengthened with a thick facing of brick-work, and painted white; for it was required to be preserved as a landmark to ships entering the roadsted. There is something extremely tranquil and pleasing in the whole of the scene,—and though the composition is simple, forms an excellent subject for a sketch.

☞ The Party may either cross the ferry with their vehicle to Bembridge—for there is a good horse-boat in attendance, and drive round Yaverland and Brading; or they may go to the latter place at once; returning over the downs to Ashey Sea-mark, which affords an almost unrivaled prospect,—and hence descend towards Ryde, making altogether a charming circuit of about sixteen miles.

## BRADING HAVEN

BRADING HAVEN, *As viewed from Bembridge Mill looking across to the Town of Brading, Nunwell, &c.* ISLE OF WIGHT.

Exhibits during high water the beautiful appearance of an extensive lake: but at the recess of the tide, a mere waste of sand and ooze, comprehending above 800 acres.

As the sea comes through a very narrow inlet at St. Helen's, several unsuccessful attempts have been made to recover from its usurpation so valuable a tract of land:—in 1630 the famous Sir H. Middleton was engaged, and indeed succeeded for a short time, by means of a bank of peculiar construction. But the sea brought up so much sand, ooze, and weeds, as to choke up the passage for the discharge of the fresh water, which accumulating, in a wet season and a spring-tide, made an irreparable breach, and thus ended an experiment which *then* cost altogether about £7000. "And after all, the nature of the ground did not answer the expectations of the undertakers; for though that part adjoining Brading proved tolerably good, nearly one-half of it was found to be a light running sand." But it should be observed, that previous to the above attempt, several of the rich meadows contiguous to the haven were at different times taken in.

One circumstance was very remarkable: namely, A WELL, cased with stone, was discovered near the middle of the haven;—an incontestible evidence, that at some remote period, the spot was in a very different condition.

To the very remarkable CHANGE which appears (by the discovery of a well,) to have taken place in the condition of the haven—and the threatened existence of St. Helen's Church, from the "encroachment of the sea,"—we beg to call the attention of our more reflecting readers. History and tradition are silent as to the cause; and the popular opinion of the present day briefly dismisses the question by ascribing it to an increased elevation of the sea. But this hypothesis is not supported by the appearance of the coast immediately to the westward of the haven, where some creeks or inlets *have become dry*; a circumstance which induced the Rev. P. Wyndham, who wrote almost the first intelligent Guide to the island, to conclude that there actually had been a secession of tides in this quarter; yet, singular enough, he makes no allusion either to the haven or the church. Now as there is really no evidence whatever in the neighbourhood that would lead us to suppose in the slightest degree, that the sea has encroached upon the land *by its gaining a higher* GENERAL *level* (an idea deprecated by many eminent geologists), we must take the alternative in accounting for the phenomenon, and infer that the land of the haven must have SUNK at some very distant period, and that more recently, the same fate attended the foundations of the church, which certainly could not have been originally built so very close to the water's edge, as to be constantly enveloped in sea-foam during every fresh breeze from the east.

Analagous to the above mutation in the state of the land, is the following singular fact related by Sir Rd. Worsley, of Appuldurcombe, who, living as it were on the spot, was not likely to be imposed upon. The reader is to picture to himself three very high downs standing nearly in a line,—St. Catharine's, Week, and Shanklin: the latter, when Sir Richard wrote the account in 1781, he guessed to be about 100 feet higher than Week Down, but which "was barely visible" over the latter from St. Catharine's, in the younger days of many of the old inhabitants of Chale, and who had also been told by their fathers that at one time Shanklin could be seen only from the top of the beacon on St. Catharine's. "This testimony, if allowed," says the worthy baronet, "argues either a sinking of the intermediate down, or a rising of one of the other hills, the causes of which are left for philosophical investigation:" and so with respect to the haven and the church, we leave it as a curious question to amuse our scientific friends—whether it is the sea that has risen, or the land which has subsided?

## BEMBRIDGE.

☞ *This is a peninsula about three miles long by one broad, terminating abruptly on the sea-side in a range of* SUBLIME CHALK PRECIPICES. *The part easily accessible to strangers is White-cliff Bay, two miles from the ferry.*

On account of the inconvenient situation of Bembridge as to the usual *routes*, it is not so much visited as Freshwater, whose precipices are on rather a grander scale, and the most celebrated in Great Britain of this magnificent species of coast scenery. For this reason, and also as the cliffs of both places agree almost precisely in their geological character (for they are but the termini of the same chain of hills), we shall merge the *general* description of the former in that of the latter; but we would advise the stranger who may sojourn at Ryde, by all means to visit Bembridge, if he should decline going to Freshwater; and if in a good boat on a fine day, so much the better,—he will be well gratified with the *brilliant* spectacle which these noble *"white cliffs of Albion"* present.

Before the year 1830, Bembridge seemed to be shut out from intercourse with the world: it was very rarely visited; possessed no facilities of communication; and had no charms to call the traveller aside from the routine track. But owing to the WISE and spirited exertions of a resident gentleman, it was soon rendered a populous village.

Among the first improvements was the erection (by public subscription) of a handsome little church for the accommodation of the inhabitants, who before had no place of episcopalian worship nearer than Brading: the next consideration was the establishment of a horse-boat, and other regular means of passage across the haven:— land was sold off on eligible terms for building; several tasty villas were soon erected, and ample shrubberies formed:—new roads were projected, the old ones widened and repaired, and travelling altogether rendered more agreeable. A respectable Hotel was also built at the same time, near the beach.

The face of the country about Bembridge is pleasant enough, being agreeably checquered by grove and meadow, cultivation and open pasturage: but it is THE SURROUNDING PROSPECT which yields the chief pleasure. The situation of the Church and other principal buildings, is sufficiently evident to the visitor from St. Helen's, or as he crosses the ferry.

The chalk precipices of Bembridge are named *the Culvers*, from the circumstance it is said, of their having been the haunt of immense numbers of wild pigeons; and they are now, as has been already mentioned (p. 21), resorted to in the summer months by prodigious flights of various sea-fowl. There is a small cavern called HERMIT'S HOLE in the face of the cliff, about thirty feet from the top; the descent to it however is steep and narrow, and it is comparatively but seldom visited.

BEMBRIDGE LEDGE is a dangerous reef of rocks, stretching out into the sea a considerable distance: a floating beacon-light called "the Nab" is always moored within a short distance, to warn ships of their position.

YAVERLAND. This is a straggling village near the sea-shore, between Brading and Sandown Fort. The little parish-church and the adjoining mansion (now converted into a farm house,) exhibit a venerable appearance, and being surrounded by groves of magnificent elms, the whole presents one of the prettiest *rural* scenes in the island; and to the amateur of sketching, it must prove a treat. The Parsonage too will be admired for its appropriate character and pleasant situation.—Passing a few scattered cottages, our road will be on the pebbly beach to ...

## SANDOWN,

Altogether an extensive village, containing several new houses built near the sea-shore, intended for letting as summer lodgings: some of them are large and splendidly furnished: and enjoy a beautiful view of the British Channel, the dazzling cliffs of Bembridge, and the range of coast for two or three miles in the direction of Shanklin. There is a church, newly erected in the upper part of the village: and a neat inn on the beach.

Midway between Sandown and Shanklin we pass through LAKE, a pretty hamlet, having a few cottages that let occasionally for lodgings during the summer months.

## BRADING

Consists of one long, ancient street (through which is the chief thoroughfare from Ryde to Shanklin and the Undercliff,) and a few good houses recently built on the outskirts: it lies about half a mile from the haven; and still retains some of the privileges of an ancient borough. The Church is considered the oldest in the island; as it was certainly in existence early in the eighth century, though some date its erection so high as the sixth, and contend that the first islanders converted to Christianity were here baptized. On account of its antiquity, the numerous relics which it contains, together with the many well written inscriptions to be found on the tombstones in the cemetery (the most noted of which perhaps is the one erected to the memory of "Little Jane,") it is very frequently visited by parties making the southern tour. The surrounding country too is agreeably varied by wood and water, arable and pasture, and a very fine outline of hill and dale.

To return to Ryde or Newport over the downs from Brading, will be found exceedingly interesting to those strangers who delight in the contemplation of grand prospects, and a most fertile and well cultivated country:—having no objection at the same time to a *hilly* road as the price of their enjoyment, and which *we* call the most beautiful in the island.

But as artists are often enraptured with passages of scenery that to others prove comparatively uninteresting, we subjoin a sketch by Sir H. ENGLEFIELD, showing the deep interest and pleasure the surrounding landscapes are capable of affording:—

"To enjoy in all its glory, the complete view of the northern tract, which in detail presents so many separate beauties, we must ascend the chalk range that rises immediately from the woods of Nunwell. When the weather is clear, it is impossible to describe the magnificent scene which these hills command, from Brading Downs, by Ashey Sea-mark, and soon quite to Arreton chalk-pit.

"To the *north*, the woodlands form an almost continued velvet carpet of near 10,000 acres, broken only by small farms, whose thatched buildings relieve the deep tints of the forests. The Wootton River winds beautifully among them, and beyond the whole the Solent Sea spreads its waters, which in clear weather is tinged with an azure more deep and beautiful than any I ever saw. The Hampshire land rises in a succession of hills quite lost at length in blue vapour. The inland view to the *south* is far from destitute of beauty, though less striking than the northern scene. The vale between the chalk range and the southern hills is seen in its full extent: and the southern hills themselves rise to a majestic height. To the *eastward* the sea is again visible over the low lands of Sandown, and by its open expanse affords a fine contrast to the Solent Channel.

"The nearer objects on the southern slope are also very interesting: Knighton House, with its venerable grey fronts mantled with luxuriant ivy, and bosomed in the richest groves, is as beautiful at a distance, as it is interesting on a nearer approach. Arreton is also surrounded with trees, which group happily with the pretty church and an old mansion now converted into a farm: and from the western end of the downs, the country about Newport and Carisbrooke is seen to great advantage. *Such is the faint outline of a scene, which, in richness of tints, and variety of objects, surpasses anything I ever saw.*"

*Note.*—Since this was written, Knighton House has been pulled down.

*Objects between Brading and Newport.*

Our course will be for the first three miles due west. On the north side is NUNWELL, the oldest seat in the island, having been awarded by William the Conqueror to the ancestors of Sir William Oglander, the present proprietor. Noble specimens of every kind of forest-tree are to be found in the park: particularly oaks, several of which are many centuries old, the family having long employed every possible means of preserving these venerable chiefs of the grove. The house (a large, plain building,) stands at the foot of the down, and therefore is not seen from the road: but the surrounding park, woods, and farms of the estate, spread before the eye in a most beautiful style ...

"With swelling slopes and groves of every green."

ASHEY SEA-MARK is very conspicuously seen, being seated on a high down, three miles from Brading, four from Ryde, and five from Newport: it is a perfectly plain, triangular object, erected in the middle of the last century to assist pilots in navigating St. Helen's anchorage.

On the south side of the down appears the pretty village of NEWCHURCH, in the direct road from Ryde to Godshill, &c. The situation of the Church is rather romantic, being nearly on the edge of a remarkably steep sand-cliff, through which the road is cut, feathered with brushwood and several overhanging trees.

If the tourist be returning to Newport, he will pass through the long village of ARRETON, whose church stands at the foot of the down of that name: it is of considerable antiquity,—and though its style of architecture is certainly heavy, is upon the whole both picturesque and singular. Its chief internal decoration is a beautiful mausoleum to the memory of Sir Leonard W. Holmes, bart.: and in the churchyard is buried the young woman celebrated for her piety in the popular tract of "the Dairyman's Daughter."

CHAPTER III.

THE ROMANTIC SCENERY

OF THE ISLAND,

EXHIBITED ALONG THE SOUTH-EASTERN COAST, FROM

SHANKLIN TO BLACKGANG CHINE.

SHANKLIN.

THE CHINE, *a beautiful woody ravine in the sea-cliffs, is the great object of attraction; inquire the road to the beach, and you will be conducted through the scene back to the village;—of the latter, a, pretty good idea may be formed in passing through it to Bonchurch,*

Here we enter upon the romantic scenery of the island. The village is most delightfully rural, and though it has several roomy lodging-houses, and two large hotels, still, from the bold variety of the ground, and the many shrubberies and clumps of fine elm and ash trees with which it is adorned, the dwellings are so hid from one another, that in almost every point of view it has the pleasing appearance of being but a small quiet hamlet. Except in the most exposed parts, vegetation flourishes with uncommon luxuriance,—even choice exotics: we would point to the Parsonage as an instance, enveloped in myrtles that stand the rigors of winter without protection: indeed it may well be said, that almost every cottage in this beautiful spot is surrounded ...

"With fragrant turf, and flowers as wild and fair,
As ever dressed a bank, or scented summer air."

But the crowning feature from which it derives its celebrity as one of the chief curiosities of the island, is THE CHINE—a term that certainly does not convey to a stranger any idea of the scene: it is a provincial expression for a ravine or cleft in the cliffs of the shore, and of which there are several along the coast, possessing a beauty or sublimity that renders them highly interesting.

Having reached the beach, the visitor should take a short walk under the towering sandrock precipices which range to the right and left for several miles, before he enters the Chine. Nowhere on the coast of the island is there a more charming stretch of shore,—for the sand is of a cool dark color, *firm enough for wheel-carriages and horses to be used by invalids*, and therefore proves equally alluring to the aged as to the young, to enjoy salubrious exercise and recreation; it extends northward to Sandown—about two miles; its monotony being broken by occasional pools of sea-water, and a sprinkling of weed-covered rocks.

THE CHINE.

SHANKLIN CHINE, ISLE OF WIGHT. (*Descent to the Beach.*)

At the foot of the cliff stands a fisherman's cottage, which may attract our attention from its picturesque situation.

The first view of the Chine from the beach is not the most favorable: as the eye of the spectator is much too low to comprehend all the deep and bold windings of the chasm, which contribute so essentially to its romantic effect: but, gradually ascending by a narrow path, we soon open a wider view, and should then pause, to contemplate it on every side. We see suspended on the opposite slope, the humble ale house, resting

"Beneath an aged oak's embowering shade."

Just below it, a pretty rose-mantled cottage: and not far off, the gable end of a gentleman's villa, so prominently seated near the margin of the precipice, as to completely overlook the awful abyss. This view is altogether picturesque and animated: for the foreground is exceedingly bold,—and the prospect of Sandown Bay and the sublime cliffs of Bembridge, give wonderful brilliancy and interest to the perspective.

As we advance, the scene becomes increasingly romantic, especially when we are about half-way through it: for the deep sides of the chasm so fold into one another as to exclude all prospect, and yet afford a great diversity of coloring, light, and shade; the one side being beautifully hung with indigenous trees or shrubs, and the uncovered portions of the cliff of a glowing tint; while the opposite side presents the contrast of a sombre hue, and is generally too steep to admit of much vegetation ever gaining a permanent footing. Nor is the most critical eye annoyed by the indications of unnecessary artificial improvements—which so often tend to destroy the delightful robe of simplicity that such scenes of Nature's creation wear, *when they are fortunate enough to escape the infliction of man's refinements.*

"Still slowly climb the many-winding way,
And frequent turn to linger as you go."

We now approach the waterfall, at the HEAD OF THE CHINE; and should there have been lately any heavy rains, it forms a noble cascade of about 30 feet; but after a continuance of dry weather, it is reduced to a scanty rill.

Ascending by a rude path cut in the side of the cliff, we pass through a rustic wicket, and take our leave of this celebrated scene, which has no doubt been formed by the slow operation of the streamlet in the course of many ages, insignificant as it may appear to a casual visitor in the middle of summer. The Chine of Blackgang is indebted for its origin to a similar cause: and this of Shanklin would have gone on rapidly increasing, had not the proprietor resorted to the aid of masonry, draining, piling, &c. to arrest in some measure its further progress towards the village.—See p. 33 of the "Vectis Scenery" for a full account of the formation of the Chines.

The sides of this chasm are about 200 feet in perpendicular height, and perhaps 300 wide at the top, near the beach, gradually diminishing towards the Head or waterfall, where the sides are perpendicular, and only a few yards asunder.

The earthy precipices between Shanklin and Luccombe Chines are called DUNNOSE,—they form the southern termination of Sandown Bay, which is a beautiful stretch of shore of above five miles in extent, bounded on the north by the white cliffs of Bembridge.

As we pursue our tour we can trace the course of the Chine (above the head), by the freshness and luxuriant growth of the trees that stand on its narrow banks: and just as we approximate the little parish-church, pass over a bridge thrown across it—but the streamlet itself is almost hidden by wild brushwood and aquatic weeds. The spring-head is a little above the church.

SHANKLIN CHURCH, I.W. *And the Road leading to Luccombe & the Undercliff*

The Plate represents the church, and a remarkable portion of the road on quitting the village for the back of the island; it is seen ascending circuitously the side of a steep down, between a hanging copse and several groups of the finest ash trees,—one of which (on the left-hand,) has long been celebrated for its amplitude and beauty.

It is quite impossible for language to convey more than a faint idea of the magnificent and interesting prospect which gradually opens to view as the traveller ascends the mountain ridge: the British Channel spreads its blue waters as the boundary on the one side; the greatest portion of the island recedes in the most charming gradations on the other: and the Solent Channel presents the animated appearance of a noble river, crowded with ships of every description; while the opposite coast of Hampshire and Sussex may be traced more or less distinctly for 70 or 80 miles.

A series of pasturing downs stretch for several miles nearly parallel with the sea-coast: of these the nearest is Shanklin—its northern slope being abruptly broken by a fine range of cliff, composed chiefly of gray free-stone feathered by hanging woods, and on the edge of this beautiful precipice stand some very picturesque ruins called ...

## COOKE's CASTLE,

COOKE's CASTLE. *An ancient ruin on the Appuldurcombe Estate—Isle of Wight.*

Which being seen from a considerable distance in various directions, and never before published, appeared to the Artist to well merit a sketch. Sir Richard Worsley, in his History of the Isle of Wight, states it to be the "ruin of an ancient castle" (though it has been said that it was built as an object of view from Appuldurcombe House); but whether artificial, or really a relic of antiquity, is of little importance, while it proves so conspicuous an ornament to the scene.

## LUCCOMBE CHINE

Is another chasm in the sea-cliffs, similar to Shanklin in its character, but on a very inferior scale: and therefore is seldom visited by those in a vehicle who have little time to spare. But many walk from Shanklin to it, either on the beach (if the tide be ebbing), or by a foot-path near the edge of the cliffs, the distance being about two miles: either way is extremely pleasant. A few houses and cottages scattered about, serve to enliven the scene.

We now approach a most singular and romantic tract of the south-eastern coast, dividing the claim of *interest* even with the sublime scenery at the west end of the island: we mean ...

## THE UNDERCLIFF,

Which commences at East End, and terminates at Blackgang Chine, an extent of above eight miles, averaging about one mile's breadth: and bounded on the land-side by a towering ridge of perpendicular stone cliffs, or precipitous chalky hills; presenting in many parts the venerable time-worn appearance of some ancient fortress. Between this craggy ridge and the sea-cliffs, every spot bears the striking impress of some violent convulsion, such in fact as would be produced by an earthquake: but in proportion to the time that shall have elapsed, so all the more rugged marks of devastation are either obliterated by the liberal hand of Nature, or converted into positive beauties. Originally the whole of this tract, or nearly so, was rock resting on a sort of loose marly foundation: this being perpetually exposed to the undermining action of the sea at its foot; accelerated in wet seasons by the marle being rendered soft and yielding,—it is evident that, sooner or later, such a foundation would give way to the immense superincumbent pressure, and be attended with all the direful effects of a real earthquake.

Most probably other subsidences will yet take place, until more of the oozy, sliding foundation shall be removed, and its place occupied by a sufficient quantity of fallen rock, as will secure the stability of the ground; as we find to be the case for the greater part of this singular tract, which has certainly been in a state of repose for seven or eight centuries at least. Fragments of the cliff are indeed frequently shivered off, but rarely or never attended with any very injurious consequences: it is those extensive *landslips* which are alarming, when many acres of valuable land are completely overturned and laid waste in a few hours. The huge masses of solid rock thus torn and dashed about, produce the grandest scenes of terror: but are at the same time the source of those singular beauties—that variety of fractured cliff and broken ground, which are the greatest ornaments of this romantic country.

### EAST END.

☞ *The Tourist ought, if possible, to walk through this very romantic scene, and if in a vehicle, be upon his guard that the driver does not hurry him by it, as is often the case.*

Here, as we have said before, the Undercliff commences: and as soon as the stranger has nearly compassed the valley of Luccombe, he should particularly enquire for the spot which is the entrance to this romantic scene ...

"Where twines a path in shadow hid,
Round many a rocky pyramid."

The distance is only a mile: the carriage in the mean time may proceed on to Bonchurch. But should the party decline the walk, they ought at least to alight, and advance near enough to the edge of the precipice, to have a view of the interesting scene below; and they must bear in mind, that though it lies within a few yards of the road, yet *to a person passing by,* there is no indication of its being so near.

The great interest of East End arises partly from its present wild character, and partly from its being the scene of the latest formidable landslips that have occurred in the island. In the year 1810, a founder took place which destroyed about twenty acres of land: this was followed by another, eight years after, that ruined in one night at least thirty acres more: at which time above twenty full-grown trees were uprooted, and several of them completely buried in the awful wreck. It therefore affords the inquisitive traveller the best opportunity of examining the cause of the peculiar character of this part of the island.

## BONCHURCH.

☞ *Formerly this was one of the most romantic scenes in the island, but has lately been converted into a fashionable village. Amidst a profusion of new houses, more or less tasty in their style—a villa, called* EAST DENE, *and the neighbouring old* CHURCH, *are all that will here particularly call the stranger from the carriage-road.*

In the year 1834, this beautiful spot was advertised to be sold off in small lots for building 18 or 20 villas!—a circumstance much regretted by the admirers of the peculiar scenery of the Undercliff, which was exhibited here in its utmost perfection. Nearly the whole of the land is now disposed of; some of the houses were built for the purpose of letting lodgings; one has been opened as a first-rate Hotel; but the greater number are private residences,—and certainly it must prove a most enviable retreat for families or invalids during the winter months. It is impossible for any spot to be better adapted for a number of houses being built in a comparatively small compass: for the whole of the ground is so romantically tossed about by the sportive hand of Nature,—presenting here a lofty ridge of rocks, there a woody dell adorned with a purling stream or a limpid pool, that most of the houses are completely hid from each other's view.

From the bad taste which too generally prevails—we mean the *vanity of glare*—the affectation of *elegance*,—so frequently carried out at the expense of all propriety, we were not without apprehension that many of the gentry at Bonchurch would also neglect the essential rule, that *the peculiar character of every scene demands an* APPROPRIATE STYLE *in building and decoration*; for it avails little to have ivy-mantled rocks and mossy cliffs, the sunny knoll and the shady glen, with their groves and streams,—if the Genius of the spot be not consulted, and HARMONY made the rule of every innovation and improvement. In a word, it is too often in building as in dress, that many persons resort to show and refinement as the surest means of attracting the world's admiration for their superior taste and rank! But in justice to the Gentlemen who have located in this fairy-land, we must acknowledge that they for the most part avoided (as far as was possible), disturbing the natural beauties of the place, and have studied to make their happy retreats ...

> "Smile with charms
> CONGENIAL TO THE SOIL, and all its own:
> For Ornament
> When foreign or fantastic, never charmed."

☞ The reader who may feel an interest on this subject is referred to pp. 36 and 43 of the *"Vectis Scenery."*

The most delightful residence at Bonchurch is called EAST DENE: the beauty of its locality is unrivaled; the exterior of the house in a chaste style; and the interior fitted-up and furnished at a great expense in the antique mode of the 16th century.

## THE PARISH CHURCH OF BONCHURCH ISLE OF WIGHT

The Tourist should certainly visit the old Church, which stands near the shore, and not far from the road, though concealed from it by a lofty ridge of the fallen cliff: it is of simple construction, but beautifully canopied by a grove of magnificent elms, and is supposed to have been built in the 11th century, — which is taken as a proof that this part of the Undercliff was certainly in a state of repose at the time of its erection; and has undoubtedly remained so ever since. Still, we cannot question for a moment, but this spot must have been in some previous age (judging from analogy,) subjected to the same catastrophes which we have witnessed even in our own time in its immediate neighbourhood at East End. There is also a new Church, of a neat design, beautifully nestled amongst the rocks in the higher part of the village.

As ROCK, in this part of the island, constitutes the chief source of picturesque effect, it would be an omission not to point out two crags which have gained quite a celebrity for their age and beauty: the first is *Hadfield's Look-out*, boldly rising from the road; the other a prominence in the face of the upper range of precipices, called *the Pulpit Rock*: the former has generally the appendage of a flag-staff, — the latter a rude cross, in unison with its name.

72

The road through the valley of Bonchurch presents a most enchanting scene: shaded by noble trees; and edged by bold rocky knolls,—and a small pellucid lake and stream, beyond which appears a romantic tract of broken ground and wild brushwood, backed by the venerable grey land-cliff and the lofty brow of St. Boniface Down. On emerging from this beautiful spot, we have on our right a genteel residence called ST. BONIFACE HOUSE, situated close at the foot of the high down which gives the name; built in a very chaste rural style; and embellished by some noble trees, and a sparkling rill.

We now open a general view of the fast-improving town of ...

## VENTNOR.

☞ *This is the chief resting-place between Shanklin and Niton. The* CHURCH, *and the* COVE, *are the most interesting features.*

Ventnor has risen into importance with a rapidity greater than any other place in the island: for as late as the year 1830 it numbered but about half-a-dozen cottages, one hotel, a small inn, and the accompaniment of a humble grist-mill, so necessary in a *retired hamlet* as this was *then*. But such has since been the eagerness for building, that land for the purpose which was at that time sold for £100 per acre, soon advanced to 300 or £400; latterly the price has risen at the rate of 800 to £1000 per acre for the more eligible sites. And at present there are three first-rate hotels and several minor inns; well stocked shops in almost every line of business: and medical men established on the spot. Several streets of considerable extent are completed, others are rapidly progressing; and much has also been done in the way of public improvements, such as paving, lighting, &c. The new Esplanade, on the beach, cannot fail to prove a delightful convenience both to the inhabitants and visitors at Ventnor.

It is greatly indebted for its prosperity to Dr. Clarke's popular Treatise, to which we have already referred (p. 16,) when speaking of the climate generally. Its progress was still more accelerated by the interest which the proprietor of Steephill Castle, John Hambrough, esq., took in its success, by erecting a handsome church, a large free-school, parsonage, &c.

Building being still carried on with undiminished speculation, the general appearance of the town must be consequently anything but agreeable—nor has there been the lapse of sufficient time for the growth of the shrubberies (however genial the climate,) to attain that size which would afford the relief of even a partial screen. Little therefore can be particularized under the present *changing aspect* of the place.

Among the buildings which attract attention in entering by the old road, are the connected range called St. Boniface Terrace, occupying a commanding situation, and the houses concurring in one general design: and below, some extensive erections, of rather a novel appearance to the untraveled eye, being strictly in imitation of the airy and picturesque style of the Italian villa.

The somewhat confused appearance of Ventnor is no doubt owing to its unexpected advance having prevented the adoption of any uniform ground-plan, as would no doubt have been done could the proprietor of the land have foreseen the magnitude to which the place was so soon to extend,—for in this respect a considerable improvement is visible in the latest-erected part of the town. The most regularly laid-out streets are near the shore: and one branch-road runs by the edge of the sea-cliffs for about half a mile towards Bonchurch, thus affording the houses an uninterrupted view of the sea.

To JOHN HAMBROUGH *Esq. of Steephill Castle, in the Isle of Wight, This view of* ST. CATHERINE'S CHURCH, *erected by him at* VENTNOR, *is most respectfully inscribed by His much obliged humble servant, GEORGE BRANNON.*

ST. CATHARINE'S CHURCH is a beautiful feature in every respect, both in its exterior and interior, being the neatest in the island: and situated as it is on a commanding knoll nearly in the middle of the town, affords an admirable relief to the whole scene, by arresting the eye from the scattered glare of the surrounding slate-roofed and white-walled buildings, — which are almost the universal character of the houses.

The COVE presents at certain times a very animated and engaging picture: fishermen preparing for or returning from their voyage; invalids and other respectable parties sauntering or reclining on the sunny beach: some reading, others amused in listening to, and watching the curling waves expire at their feet in spreading foam. The material of the shore is principally fine shingle, or very small pebbles, among which particles are frequently picked up, possessing a brilliancy that has gained for them the title of "Isle of Wight diamonds;" and though they may be comparatively of inferior value in point of intrinsic quality,—still, the *interest* taken in searching for them must prove a source of the most agreeable employment to those visitors whose health precludes any exercise of a more active nature.

ST. BONIFACE DOWN, which forms a green back-ground to the view, is also an object of interest (at least with artists or amateurs of sketching,) that ought not to be passed by unnoticed. It is exceedingly steep: has a never-failing spring on its lofty summit, and is often cheerfully sprinkled with sheep, of the South-down breed, safely nibbling the close herbage on its precipitous side.

Speaking of the down, we should deserve to be censured by those of our elderly readers who may have been to Ventnor ere it reached the magnitude of a town, not to inform them, that *the then only Hotel* (so beautifully seated close at the foot of the hill,) *is no longer a place of public accommodation*; the license has been transferred. Many were the respectable parties of the olden time who used to amuse themselves with the attempt to gain the summit of the down,—sometimes successfully, but more frequently at the expense of a rather too precipitate descent, to the no small diversion of their friends who had less daring to make the experiment. In this age of refinement, such displays of rural agility would be regarded as "utterly vulgar!" there are however more circuitous and accessible paths by which we may reach the eminence, and hence enjoy a most delightful prospect.

In concluding this brief notice of Ventnor, it would be very unfair to Dr. Clarke, not to mention the fact, that he was decidedly opposed to the residences of invalids (with pulmonary consumption) being accumulated together *"in the form of a Town;"* he recommends that a number of *detached* houses should be built along the Undercliff, each surrounded with the protection of a garden-wall and a few trees. But, begging the Doctor's pardon, we heartily rejoice that his advice could not be acted upon to any considerable extent (except at Ventnor and Bonchurch); because fortunately the most eligible and attractive spots in this romantic district are in the holding of gentlemen who have chosen such for their *private* residences: and certainly, if selfishness was ever pardonable, it is so in this instance;

nay, for our part, we really congratulate the public, that the spirit of exclusiveness so widely exists in this happy region of the sublime and beautiful. For what a lamentable transformation it would prove of the natural character of the scenery, to have many large and often glary houses obtruding upon the eye in every direction! banishing all the *wildest* and most interesting local beauties, for domestic convenience or fantastic embellishment! Where then would be the attraction to call the thousands annually to our romantic isle? Where those UNIQUE LANDSCAPES which now constitute its proudest charm?

And after all, the Doctor's objection to a residence in town, is largely compensated for in the case of Ventnor, by the many advantages afforded to invalids, that could be procured only in a populous place: such for instance as regular stage-coaches running to and from Ryde and other places; a good landing-place; bathing-machines; a post-office and reading-rooms; the location of several apothecaries and eminent physicians: tradesmen of almost every description; and the facility of enjoying society in the dullest winter months.

Westward of Ventnor, we have a sudden and most agreeable transition from the glare of the town to a quiet picture of rural scenery, broken only by two or three cottages neatly built in the antique style; this is the commencement of the property of Mr. Hambrough (of Steephill Castle), which extends to St. Lawrence, the estate of Earl Yarborough; succeeded by Old Park; and near Niton, the seats of Mrs. Arnold, Sir W. Gordon, and Mrs. Vine: altogether a delightful distance of above four miles; which we hope will long escape any desecration of its beauties by the operations of building speculators.

## APPULDURCOMBE.

This splendid seat, from its proximity to the Undercliff, is most frequently embraced either in the south-eastern or the continued

Tour, in preference to giving it a separate day: therefore here is perhaps the best place for its notice, especially as the regular road from Ventnor to Newport passes close by: and as it is only two miles from the former town. It is thus described by Sir Richard Worsley, in his "History of the Isle of Wight:"

"The house is pleasantly situated about seven miles south of the town of Newport: it has four regular fronts of the Corinthian order, built of freestone; the pilasters, cornices, ballustrades, and other ornamental parts are of Portland stone; the roof is covered with Westmoreland slates. The grand entrance in the east front is through a hall 54 feet in length by 24 in breadth, adorned with eight beautiful columns of the Ionic order resembling porphyry. On this floor are several handsome apartments, containing many valuable portraits, and other good paintings; the offices are very commodious, and on the first and attic stories are upwards of twenty bed-chambers with dressing-rooms. The house was begun by Sir Robert Worsley, in 1710: and completed by Sir Richard Worsley, who made considerable additions, and much improved upon the original design."

Sir Richard spent a great portion of his life in collecting the paintings and other relics of antiquity which adorn the mansion, and published a very sumptuous descriptive work, entitled "Museum Worsleyanum." The Estate descended to the Pelham family by the marriage of the Baronet's niece to the late Earl Yarborough.

The park of Appuldurcombe is extensive; and the soil being extremely rich, supports a great number both of deer and cattle, — the former of which is nowhere else to be found in the island. At the back of the mansion rises a lofty hill, whose sides are hung with groves of noble beech, interspersed with many venerable oaks. On the summit is an obelisk, originally seventy feet high, built of Cornish granite, to the memory of Sir Robert Worsley: but of late years it has suffered severely from the high winds, to the violence of which its elevated position renders it so exposed. From almost every part of this down we gain the most splendid views; below, is the rich vale of Arreton, Newchurch, and Godshill: beyond is seen on the north, Portsmouth and the neighbouring anchorages, with the wooded heights above Southampton Water; eastward are the beautiful shores of Sandown Bay; to the west the prospect is continued far beyond the white cliffs of Freshwater, by the coasts of Hants and Dorset: and on the south expands the azure horizon of the boundless ocean.

N.B. Strangers desirous of visiting Appuldurcombe, must provide themselves with tickets at the office of the stewards, Messrs. Sewell, Solicitors, Newport: the days allowed are Tuesdays and Fridays, between the hours of 11 and 4 o'clock.

## GODSHILL,

Bordering on Appuldurcombe Park, is a populous village, chiefly remarkable for the very picturesque situation of the Church, a large and venerable pile, which stands upon a steep hill in the centre of the village,—commanding such an extensive and beautiful prospect as will of itself repay the tourist for the trouble of ascending. The interior of the church is enriched by several interesting monuments, ancient and modern, in memory of the various possessors of the Appuldurcombe estates,—the most sumptuous being that to Sir J. Leigh and his lady, whose marble effigies are canopied by a beautifully ornamented arch; and the massive tomb of Sir Richard Worsley, which occupies the south transept, where a colored window is placed to give it greater effect.—Godshill has a small country inn called the Griffin.

The distance from Ventnor to Godshill is four miles:—and thence to Newport, six: the country is well-cultivated, but presents no object to call for particular notice: we pass the hamlet of ROOKLEY: and the villas of PIDFORD and STANDEN.

WHITWELL is a very retired village, winding between Godshill and Niton: and having a church of some antiquity.

Returned to the Undercliff, the next place in our route which boasts of superior scenic beauty is ...

STEEPHILL,

STEEPHILL, UNDERCLIFF, ISLE OF WIGHT.

Where a splendid CASTLE was erected in the year 1833, by J. Hambrough, esq. (thence often called after his name), on a broad terrace of rock that rises almost perpendicularly from the present road: and here it may not be quite uninteresting to state—at least to some of our friends who used to visit the island years ago, that the castle occupies the very site of the once-noted Cottage of the late Earl

Dysart, and which was for many years that nobleman's favorite retreat. Steephill was then a most charming rural hamlet; but the cottages are removed (much to the advantage of the tenants), to afford a scope in the grounds corresponding with the dignity of the new mansion. Rustic simplicity and the wilder graces have given way to elegance and polished decoration: but whether the alteration

"Adds beauties to what Nature plann'd before,"

Is merely a question of taste, on which we shall not presume to decide: various are the opinions,

—"And many a stranger stops,
With curious eye, to censure or admire."

As the public are now excluded from the garden and pleasure-grounds, it is rather difficult to get a good view of the castle; the best places however are ... a lofty knoll or promontory on the opposite side of the road,—and a rocky mound near THE CAVE, which is in the face of the sea-cliffs, marked by a flag-staff; and there is, close by, a path to the beach. Half an hour's saunter would be quite sufficient to enable a visitor to judge of the beauty of the scene—which at one time procured it the title of *Queen of the Undercliff.* If but five minutes can be spared, the tourist ought to quit his vehicle, and reach the brow of the promontory above alluded to, were it only for the sake of the delightful prospect which it affords.

The coast of Steephill forms a pleasant little cove or bay, with remarkably bold and picturesque headlands: and the place altogether equals any part of the Undercliff in its natural embellishment of rich groves and sparkling streams, mossy rocks, and broken ground.

DESCRIPTION OF THE CASTLE.—In the design of this stately edifice, it appears to have been the aim of the architect to combine, as much as possible, all the internal advantages of a plain mansion, with the commanding form and embellished detail which usually characterize a castellated structure. It is not therefore open to an

81

objection which lies against many of the most picturesque specimens of this dignified style of building—that internal convenience was sacrificed to the production of bold and pleasing contrasts in the face of the exterior: or that it was the growth of successive improvements. Indeed, both inside and out, all appears to be handsomely proportioned and well-arranged; while in any point of view the whole presents an aspect of elegant simplicity.—The general form of the castle is an oblong; and the most prominent features ... one majestic square tower which springs from about the centre of the north side; another tower of an octagon form at the south-eastern angle; and a beautiful hall-entrance on the east. The predominant tint is a dark grey: but the battlements, quoins, and mouldings, are of a light warm color, resembling the Bath stone. This opposition of tints has a most pleasing, chaste effect, when closely examined: but at a distance the whole melts into a sober hue, like the grey impression of time, and hence harmonizes the more sweetly with the surrounding scenery. Both kinds of stone were procured on the spot.—The architect was the late Mr. James Sanderson, of Ryde.

*Remarks on the Exclusion of Strangers from most of the Gentlemen's Seats.*—However provoking it may prove to many visitors when making the tour of the island, to be shut out from a view of some of the most charming seats, still it may be justified in a considerable degree; and we feel it our duty to repeat what we have stated elsewhere, that we know several gentlemen who would freely open their gates to respectable visitors, provided they could be assured of every party being contented with a general view of the local beauties, without indulging a too prying curiosity; and at the same time would *refrain from plucking choice flowers, fruits, and shrubs,* many of which may perhaps have been cultivated by the hands of the owner with an affection of no little solicitude and pride; and of course it is not always convenient to keep a person merely to act as an attendant. But a more decisive reason with many gentlemen who love retirement is, that from the island becoming every year more and more attractive with pleasure-parties, an *unlimited admission* of strangers would at once annihilate all the charms of rural seclusion; it would in fact be converting the flowery walks of a quiet country-villa into as giddy a promenade as almost any popular tea-garden in the suburbs of the metropolis. Still however, speaking generally, it requires only some slight grounds of introduction: and in the absence of the family there is of course less difficulty,—it being then a privilege often given to the servants.

---

## ST. LAWRENCE.

☞ *The* CHURCH, *here, is from its diminutiveness, quite an object of curiosity; and the stranger will also notice* THE WELL, *on the road-side; but the* VILLA *and* COTTAGE *are both secluded from public view.*

---

"Here lawns, and groves, and op'ning prospects break
With sweet surprize upon the wand'ring eye:—
While through romantic scenes and hanging woods.
And valleys green, and rocks, and hollow dales,
We rove enchanted."

The scenery of St. Lawrence is a singular union of the cultivated with the wild and romantic—a pleasing interchange of the elegance of splendid retirement with the unobtrusive dwellings of laboring peasants, scattered amidst sheltering groves and ivy-covered rocks. Here the Rt. Hon. Earl Yarborough has ...

"A country-cottage—near a chrystal flood,
A winding valley, and a lofty wood;"

Long celebrated as the favorite retreat of the late Sir Richard Worsley, of Appuldurcombe Park, who embellished it in quite a classical style—planting a vineyard, decorating the grounds with models of ancient temples, &c. The house has since been considerably enlarged, and ornamented in the old-English style with elaborate barge-boards and pinnacles. At a short distance is the recently built residence of his Lordship's brother, the Hon. Capt. C.D. Pelham, R.N.—also in the Elizabethan style. By way of contradistinction, the original is emphatically called *the Villa*, and the latter, *the Cottage*. It is much to be regretted, that the public have of late been altogether excluded from the grounds—from even walking on the edge of the sea-cliffs!

ST LAWRENCE CHURCH *UNDERCLIFF ISLE OF WIGHT*

The miniature CHURCH seldom fails of proving an amusing object with every visitor,—for it ranks among the smallest parochial places of religious worship in Great Britain: its belfry, the pretty little porch, and its several windows, are all in character; it has however lately been found necessary to lengthen the building, in consequence of the increase of population in the vicinity.

*ST LAWRENCE. — The WELL near the Marine Villa of the Right*
*Honourable Lord Yarborough. — Isle of Wight.*

THE WELL encloses a fountain of ever-running crystal water, the soft murmurs of which combine with the surrounding scene to produce the most agreeable feelings; and it is marked by so much of that beautiful simplicity which is the foundation of picturesque effect, that perhaps no other object in its charming neighbourhood, except the little church, will afford the stranger more immediate pleasure.

## THE ROAD FROM ST. LAWRENCE TO NITON.

☞ *For the succeeding mile and a half, our attention will be called to no one particular object; but we shall have the Undercliff in all its native character, a circumstance which must prove gratifying to those who admire Nature in* HER OWN *attire,*

The reader will be pleased, we have no doubt, with the following brief notice of this part of the coast, by the late celebrated Mrs. Radcliffe:—

"Oct. 15, 1811.—Passed Lord Dysart's beautiful cottage: it stands at some distance from the shore, and has several distinct roofs, well thatched: stands at the head of a winding lawn, with a fine beech-grove, and richly-colored copse. The little parish-church of St. Lawrence, perhaps the smallest in England, stands on a knoll, and terminates the cultivated valley; immediately beyond which we entered upon a scene of the wildest grandeur and solemnity. Many of the ruinous precipices of the upper cliffs project in horizontal strata, yet have perpendicular rents. Some of the shattered masses give the clearest echoes: we stood before one which responded every syllable with an exactness which was truly astonishing.—There is sometimes what may be called an amphitheatre of rock, where all the area is filled with ruins, which are however covered with verdure and underwood, that stretch up the sides with the wildest pomp: and shelter here a cottage, there a villa, among the rocky hillocks."

Passing a gentleman's residence situated below the road on our left, called OLD PARK (not from its display of sylvan honors), we should look out for a romantic ascent in the lofty cliffs called ...

### CRIPPLE-PATH:

It is worth examining, being a curious instance of the formation of the bold horizontal crags and ledges which distinguish these hoary precipices. For some distance the path is in a sunken stratum of soft freestone, while the upper ledge of more stubborn rock overhangs it several feet. Having reached the eminence by a rude winding staircase in a rent of the cliff,—we shall be well repaid for our trifling labor, by the beautiful prospect which is disclosed of the Undercliff, spread like an extensive garden immediately under our feet. Many parties walk hence on the edge of the cliffs to Niton, &c.

MIRABLES is another charming villa, through whose luxuriant plantations the road is carried for nearly half a mile, affording a most grateful shade: but, by the bye, at the expense of all prospect.

"Refreshing change, where now the blazing sun?
By short transition we have lost his glare,
And stepp'd at once into a cooler clime."

The house is secluded from our view: it is in the plain cottage style: but the grounds are not surpassed for rock and sylvan beauty by any seat on the coast.

We successively pass through the grounds, close and open, of the three following villas:

THE ORCHARD (on the same side of the road as Mirables, and like it, not open to the public view): a spacious villa in the embellished style, and the grounds immediately in front being formed into a succession of walled terraces, where the grape-vine and the peach find a congenial aspect: the coping too is adorned with a profusion of elegant vases, filled with the choicest flowers, nor is a gentle fountain wanting to complete the Italian beauty of the scene.

BEAUCHAMP, an unpretending residence in the simple cottage style, on the right-hand side of the road, proceeding to Niton: we catch a glimpse of it through the trees.

PUCKASTER COTTAGE, the property of the late James Vine, esq., remarkable for its chaste and *appropriate* design, *as a residence seated amidst colossal rocks, precipices, and wild tufted knolls.* The house, the improvements in the grounds, and every decoration, in character,— UNITY marking the whole: rather an uncommon circumstance, where there is an unceasing desire to give every grace to a favorite scene— and withal, ample scope and means to indulge the wish.

The old road now makes a sudden turn on our right, and here occurs the only considerable break in the upper boundary line of the Undercliff from one end to the other. To the left of us, a considerable extent of land has been laid out and partly disposed of, for the purpose of building on; and new roads made accordingly: but as yet however the speculation has not been carried on with much spirit.

At a short distance we come in front of the garden-wall of a gentleman's villa called WESTCLIFF, a beautiful and well-sheltered spot where the road abruptly divides, the left-hand branch pursuing the tour to Blackgang Chine, and the right to Newport through NITON, a village composed of a number of stone-built thatched cottages, some of which are furnished for lodgings; and has also a decent small inn called the White Lion. The Church is a pretty little object enough, standing at the foot of the down, over which used to be the only direct high-road to Chale and Blackgang Chine.

Continuing on towards the Chalybeate Spring, we pass Westcliff, and come to the ROYAL SANDROCK HOTEL, placed in a most beautiful and commanding situation; it will be readily distinguished by its ample verandah, mantled with the choicest creepers.—Next to the Hotel appears MOUNT CLEEVES, a respectable residence near the foot of the cliff, surrounded by huge rocks and craggy mounds:—one of these is adorned by a small obelisk that serves to mark a beautiful feature which would otherwise be overlooked. The cottage-lodge below is a remarkably pretty object.—See the Plate.

This part of the Undercliff is at once picturesque and lively; there being just sufficient houses to give the scenery a cheerful aspect, without intrenching too much on the natural beauties of the place.

We now enter on a scene which gives us a complete picture of the Undercliff in all its genuine lines,—for it was the subject of an extensive landslip in the year 1799, when a tract of about one hundred acres was disturbed, the whole sliding forward in a mass towards the sea, rifting into frightful chasms, and alternately rising and falling like the waves of the sea: a cottage was overturned, but fortunately no lives were lost.

THE UNDERCLIFF, *Between the Sandrock Hotel & the Chalybeate Spring, — affording the best idea of the romantic character of that part of the Isle of Wight.*

The annexed Plate of "the Undercliff, as it appears between the Sandrock Hotel and Blackgang Chine," is introduced in order to give an idea of the *general aspect* of this singular tract: the wall-like precipice which is the land-boundary rises abruptly on the right: the intermediate space to the sea-shore is broken into a series of craggy knolls and dells: the carriage-road threading its way between immense masses of the fallen cliff, — now conducted along the margin of a dangerous slope or precipice; and now descending into a theatre of detached rocks and wild vegetation; but even here, though the softer charms of scenery be wanting, it proves that ...

    —"Whether drest or rude,
Wild without art, or artfully subdued,
Nature in every form inspires delight."

*The individual objects in the neighbourhood of Niton, calling for particular remark, are few; notwithstanding the general aspect of the scenery is strikingly wild and sombre. The* LIGHT-HOUSE *will force itself on our attention: the* CHALYBEATE SPRING *ought not to be passed by unnoticed; but the crowning feature of the district is* BLACKGANG CHINE, *a scene of the most terrific grandeur.*

## ST. CATHARINE'S LIGHT-HOUSE.

## ST. CATHARINE'S LIGHT-HOUSE NITON, ISLE OF WIGHT.

The building of this lofty tower was commenced in the spring of 1839, and finished in the following year: the undertaking having originated in consequence of the loss of the ship *Clarendon* (see p. 85). From the frequent wrecks on this most dangerous part of the coast, it is rather surprizing that such a warning friend to the hapless mariner was not erected before: because many of the catastrophes were owing to the want of some light or signal in the night, which could be distinctly seen by seamen long ere they reached the fatal shore. It is true indeed, that between 50 and 60 years ago, a Light-house was built on the summit of St. Catharine's down, but for some reason not known to the public, it never was equipped and lighted: and was in fact very soon abandoned. It has been said that the site was too elevated, that it would be quite obscured by fogs and mists in those very seasons when its friendly ray was the most required;—it might be so, but certainly that was never proved by the experiment: and it seems strange that these grounds of objection were not suggested to the projectors in time.

The new Light-house stands near the edge of the sea-cliffs, at an elevation of about fifty feet above the beach. The stone Tower is 101 feet high from the surface of the ground, besides the lantern of about 20 feet more: and the foundation is of *solid masonry* to the depth of thirty feet! The requisite offices for the two light-keepers are built round the foot of the tower, and are comparatively low, so that at a distance the lofty fabric appears as a magnificent column, or

> "Like some tall watch-tower nodding o'er the deep,
> Whose rocky base the foaming waters sweep."

Inside the tower a broad stone staircase winds spirally to the top; and many visitors make the ascent, for the sake of the beautiful view afforded of the adjacent part of the Undercliff, as well as for examining the splendid and complicated lantern.

---

As the carriage-road now pursues its mazy course through ...

> "Crags, knolls, and mounds, confus'dly hurl'd,
> The fragments of an earlier world,"

We soon reach the locality of the SANDROCK CHALYBEATE SPRING: easily recognized by the low thatched roof of the Dispensary Cottage, that stands nearly on the brow of the cliff, as the water issues from a rock considerably below, inclosed in a plain piece of masonry. It has been proved by repeated analyses, that there is a larger proportion of iron and alumine in this than in any other mineral water yet discovered: and its medicinal properties are therefore decidedly indicated in the cure of those disorders arising from a relaxed fibre and languid circulation, such as indigestion, flatulency, nervous disorders, and debility from a long residence in hot climates.

Great improvement has taken place in the neighbourhood of the Spring, within these few years, by *extensive draining*: thus preventing the land-soaks and springs during winter from settling into frequent pools, and thereby reducing the soil to the repulsive condition of a sterile waste of quagmire and sliding rocks, and in every succeeding summer drying up into a thousand dangerous holes and fissures. The ground in fact is now sufficiently firm to invite the builder to the erection of some good houses; and the surface exhibits a healthy herbage: roads have also been made to the shore. A large and handsome-looking house, called an "Italian Villa," has been erected on the east side of the Spring,—but if the architect ever copied such for his model, he certainly should have selected a site more appropriate, that would have justified his choice of style by its genial aspect, its greenwood shades, and the vegetative luxuriance of the soil.

The shore here is called ROCKEN-END RACE, being composed of vast confused heaps of rocky fragments precipitated in the course of ages from the cliffs above, and now stretching out into the sea for nearly a mile and a half.—Between this and Freshwater lie other formidable reefs, respectively named from the nearest villages, ATHERFIELD, CHILTON, and BROOKE; they are extremely dangerous: and previously to the erection of the new Light-house, occasioned frequent shipwrecks.

BLACKGANG CHINE,

BLACKGANG CHINE, I.W. *Taken from below the new Bridge, which is a very general point of view, as the descent to the shore thence becomes more abrupt and difficult.*

"Where hills with naked heads the tempests meet—
Rocks at their sides, and torrents at their feet,"

Deservedly ranks among the most striking scenes in the island, it is the termination of the Undercliff, and of a character the very reverse of Shanklin; for all here is terrific grandeur—without a green spray or scarcely a tuft of verdure to soften its savage aspect. It differs also from that sylvan spot, in being much more lofty, abrupt, and irregular: though it does not penetrate the land so far. Both have their respective admirers: this for its awful sublimity—that for its romantic beauty.

At the head of the Chine is a spacious Hotel, close to the road, and distinguished by the name of the place.

The shelving sides of this gloomy chasm are proved to be little less than 500 feet from the beach in perpendicular height; they are in a constant state of decay—more or less considerable according to the degree of rain and frost during winter: for the same description of soil, namely, a mixture of clay and loose absorbent marle, interspersed with veins of gravel, predominate here as we have seen elsewhere in its neighbourhood. The only relief in fact to the dusky tint of the scene, is two or three horizontal strata of yellowish free-stone, which give it a step-like appearance. The most remarkable feature is a tremendous gloomy hollow or cave, scooped out of the cliffs on the sea-shore by the united action of the waves and the stream: the latter falls over a ledge of the stubborn rock at the top, 70 feet high: and after heavy floods, forms a noble cascade of one unbroken sheet: but like others of its class, in summer fails in its amount, and often degenerates into a noiseless dribble.

Nowhere can we get a complete view of Blackgang except off on the water, which is not always practicable: certainly not in the very seasons when the whole appears with the greatest interest,—when there is a strong wind and tide setting in-shore, and the face of Nature is shrouded in deepening gloom, with perhaps some hapless vessel in danger of being wrecked,—it is then dressed in all the congenial horrors of savage sublimity.—No one, a stranger to the sea-coast, would imagine how awfully the surges lash the stony beach in tempestuous weather: the high-curling waves break with a deafening roar, and mounting the lofty cliffs in sheets of dazzling foam, are wafted in misty clouds half over the island—even to Newport, where the windows facing the south are occasionally dimmed with the saline vapors, almost to an incrustation.

The visitor will of course endeavour to descend to the shore; but this is sometimes attended with considerable fatigue and difficulty, after wet weather, to those who are delicate and infirm. For this reason, we have taken our sketch from near the new bridge, to which the descent from the hotel is generally easy: and from which the visitor may gain such a view as will enable him to form a very good idea of the whole scene. The windings of the Chine commence a little below the Hotel, which (as already stated) stands at least 500 feet above the beach.

From the proximity of several newly erected villas and lodging-houses, it ought here to be stated to the visitor, that the *true character* of the place is in consequence greatly injured: for the garish and obtrusive habitations of genteel life but ill accord with that solitary and impressive magnificence which constitutes the very interest—the sublimity and peculiarity of a silent and cheerless scene, such as formerly were the aspect and condition of Blackgang Chine and its immediate neighbourhood.

"There has long been a tradition that Blackgang Chine was once the favorite retreat of a gang of pirates, and from that circumstance its name was derived.—Without disputing the fact of its having offered occasionally concealment and a safe depository to smugglers, or even pirates for a time,—it is equally, if not more probable, that it is indebted for its very expressive appellation to its sombre coloring, and the *step-like* appearance of the strata, if the word *gang* be admitted to have the same signification as it has in a ship."

Between Blackgang and Freshwater are several other Chines on an inferior scale, partaking more or less of the same sterile aspect: such are Walpan, Whale, Compton, Cowleaze and the Shepherd's, Grange, Chilton, and Brooke: but though several of them are well entitled to notice, they are seldom visited, owing to their remoteness from the public roads.

It should be observed however, that though they possess less scenic interest than those already described,—they embrace a portion of the island most attractive to the geologist, from the circumstance of the cliffs and shores abounding in the most beautiful specimens of fossil remains.—We would moreover call the attention of those visitors who may desire to examine into the agency which has produced the chines, to the two called *Cowleaze* and *the Shepherd's*—the latter of which has been formed within the last 40 years, in consequence, it is said, of a countryman in an idle moment turning the course of the small rivulet which had hitherto run through Cowleaze. They are situated about a mile from Brixton.

## St. CATHARINE'S HILL

(In the steep side of which on the south is Blackgang Chine), is the highest in the island, or between 800 and 900 feet above the level of the sea. An ancient octagon tower stands at the top, built on the site of, or rather as an appendage to, a hermitage—originally endowed by a benevolent individual for the purpose of providing lights in dark and stormy nights:—there is also the shell of the old light-house mentioned at p. 79.

The regular carriage-road between Chale and Niton used to be over this down previous to the year 1838: and we in some measure regret (although *celerity* in travelling be now the order of the day), that it is superseded by the road then made to Blackgang: to the admirers of illimitable prospect it afforded a rich treat, "for language is scarcely adequate to describe the various beauties which present themselves from this elevated spot."

On the northern extremity of St. Catharine's down is an elegant and most conspicuous object (72 feet high,) called the ALEXANDRIAN PILLAR: the purpose of its erection is perhaps best told by the inscription itself:

*"In commemoration of the visit of his Imperial Majesty Alexander I, Emperor of all the Russias, to Great Britain in the year 1814—and in remembrance of the many happy years' residence in his dominions—this Pillar was erected by Michael Hoy."*

On the slope is a seat called the MEDINA HERMITAGE (formerly the summer-residence of the gentleman named on the pillar): the house is characterized by simplicity and neatness: and its greatest ornament is a large verandah, having a broad *trellis* roof, beautifully intertwined with the sweetest varieties of climbing plants. From its very elevated situation, it commands a rich display of the country from Niton to Newport.

## CHALE CHURCH

Must be passed in the regular tour, going to or returning from Blackgang; stands close to the road; and though simple in its architecture, has a venerable and rather picturesque appearance—especially its square tower, which proves a great relief to the flatness of the view looking westward to the Freshwater cliffs: dates its erection in the 12th century; and exposed as it is to the rage of the elements, affords an instance of the stability which characterizes the structures of antiquity.

The cemetery of Chale incloses many a shipwrecked mariner—no doubt some hundreds who were deposited, in the course of ages, without any memento whatever: but the public are now more interested, from the circumstance of the unfortunate sufferers in the wreck of the ship Clarendon being here interred,—to whose memory tombstones are erected, on which the date and other particulars of their melancholy fate are recorded.

## WRECKS ON THE SOUTHERN COAST.

We have already stated how dangerous this part of the coast is during a south or south-west wind, to vessels unmanageable in a storm: and previously to the erection of the new Light-house, few winters passed without two or more wrecks occurring between Niton and Freshwater Bay. In former times, the *waifs*, or possession of such remains of ships or their cargoes as were washed ashore, seems to have been a valued right of this, as well as some other manors in the Isle of Wight; and many tales have been told of the inhumanity of the wreckers who in those days are said to have resided in the neighbourhood,—which, if true, are strongly contrasted by the ready zeal and liberality which the present inhabitants display in assisting those unfortunates whom the furious elements so often cast on this fatal shore.

Of the numerous vessels which have been lost here in our own time, the largest was perhaps the *Carn-brea Castle* East Indiaman, in July 1829: she left Spithead at nine o'clock in the morning, and about six hours afterwards struck on the rocks near Mottistone: the weather being fine, her crew and passengers easily reached the shore. The size of the ship, and the remarkable circumstances under which she was lost, attracted a considerable number of visitors to the spot,—as she was not immediately broken up, though all hopes of removing her were soon abandoned.

A far more disastrous wreck was that of the CLARENDON, a West India trader of 350 tons, which took place on the 11th of October, 1836: and will be remembered with increased interest, as the acknowledged fact of her loss being mainly attributable to the want of some warning beacon on the land, led almost directly to the erection of the splendid light-house at Niton. She had 11 passengers, male and female, and 17 seamen on board: her cargo consisted of sugar, rum, molasses, and turtle; she was heavily laden, and had been about six weeks on her voyage. The preceding evening was fine, and the breeze favorable, and the passengers retired to rest in fancied security, with the pleasing hope of safely reaching their destination on the following day. After midnight the wind increased; but though the ship drove rapidly before it, no danger was perceived till about day-break,—when, already in the surf, there was no longer a possibility of escape. The crew immediately proceeded to set all sail the storm would permit, in hopes of weathering the point; but their gallant efforts could not long delay the fate of the doomed vessel, she continued to drift towards the beach, on which she struck a little before six o'clock, and within five minutes was totally demolished. It would be a useless attempt to describe the horrors of that short but fearful period: all that could be gathered from the statements of the survivors was, that she twice touched the ground lightly, forward, at which time all her people were assembled on the deck; and presently one mountain wave hurled her broadside on the beach with such stupendous force, that the huge hull at once parted into a thousand fragments! The frightful brevity of the whole catastrophe prevented any measures being taken for the relief of the passengers and crew, although the ship was scarcely twice her own length from the cliff; and all perished except the mate and two seamen, who were rescued by the courageous exertions of some countrymen who had hastened to the spot as soon as dawn disclosed the inevitable danger of the vessel.—For some hours afterwards a hideous spectacle was here presented,—the naked and mangled bodies of the unfortunate sufferers, with the remains of the vessel and cargo, were tossed about in dire confusion by the raging waves, or dashed again and again on the stony beach; but before the close of the day, most of the former had been drawn ashore, and the broken fragments of the wreck were strewed on the beach for several miles. Six of the passengers (an officer named Shore, his wife, and daughters,) were buried in Newport churchyard, where a monument has since been erected to their memory; and it is a strange fact that the premises which adjoin that cemetery on the western side, had been but a short time previously engaged for their reception by a near relative, who there anxiously awaited the ship's arrival. Most of the others (as already mentioned,) were interred at Chale.

Subsequently, the wrecks on the island coast have been less numerous, and rarely accompanied by loss of life or any other circumstance of particular interest: the case of H.M. Steam-sloop SPHYNX, however, having excited so large a share of public attention, claims a brief notice. Returning from her first voyage to Africa, she neared the coast during a thick fog about six o'clock on the morning of Jan. 16, 1847: and by the force of her engines was driven over the outer ledge (off Brooke), and firmly fixed in the clay beds within. The suddenness of the accident caused great alarm amongst her crew and passengers (300 in number): and the startling discharges of her heavy artillery quickly aroused the inhabitants for miles round: but daylight and the ebbing tide enabled her people to reach land with no great difficulty,—although a boat, sent to her from another war-steamer, capsized with the loss of seven men. For nearly two months, repeated efforts were made to extricate the Sphynx from her awkward position: and after her masts, guns, and most of her stores and machinery had been removed, and the hull itself buoyed up by a vast number of empty casks, and some decked lighters (called camels), she was at length brought off and towed into Portsmouth harbour on the 3rd. of March. Her bottom had sustained considerable injury, though much less than was expected from her having lain so long in such a situation, and during several severe gales.

The VILLAGE OF CHALE lies at the foot of St. Catharine's Hill, and comprises a considerable number of scattered cottages: none of them however deserving a stranger's notice, except perhaps the Parsonage, and the Abbey-farm-house; the latter covered with the most luxuriant ivy.

If the visitor be on his return to Newport, he will within three miles of it pass GATCOMBE, a small village, and a first rate seat: exhibiting altogether perhaps the most charming *inland* scenery in the Isle of Wight:—

"Sweet are its groves, and verdant are its fields."

The mansion is a large square edifice, extremely well-situated,—in front a fine lawn falls with an easy slope, shaded by many noble oaks and elms: and immediately behind rises a steep hill luxuriantly clothed with hanging plantations. At a short distance from the house is a small lake; and near the latter, the neat little parish-church, and the Parsonage, both beautifully embosomed in wood.

## THE ROAD TO FRESHWATER-GATE.

☞ *From Chale to the celebrated Cliff's of Freshwater is about twelve miles; the first eight of which are through an agricultural district, presenting only so many agreeable pictures of rural life,—and of these the principal are* SHORWELL, NORTHCOURT, *and* BRIXTON.

"A simple scene! yet hence Brittannia sees
Her solid grandeur rise."

The fact is, the greater part of the soil is so extremely fertile, as to be employed in tillage and meadow, almost to the exclusion of woods and coppice, which constitute the chief ornaments of a landscape. We have, however, nearly the whole of the journey such a charming view of the ocean, as to compensate for the deficiency of sylvan beauties.

After passing a small church called KINGSTON, posted on a knoll, and surrounded by a few trees which bespeak their bleak exposure, we reach ...

SHORWELL,

A considerable village, about four miles from Chale, and five from Newport; it stands charmingly sheltered in a curve of the downs with a southern aspect; has a pretty church; and boasts of the finest old mansion in the island, called NORTHCOURT, built in the reign of James I. This venerable pile has lately been thoroughly repaired: a necessary operation by the bye that has stripped it for a few years of its greatest ornament—the rich drapery of ivy which invested its lofty gray walls and pinnacles: hills, clothed with hanging woods and plantations, rise boldly around it; many of the oaks and pines, luxuriating in a fertile soil and genial climate, are uncommonly fine: the grounds too are embellished with a rustic temple, and a very elegant mausoleum to the memory of Miss Bull, the daughter of a former owner,—the whole scene indeed is replete with architectural and sylvan beauties. There are in the neighbourhood two other ancient manorial residences, named Westcourt and Woolverton, now converted into farm-houses: and the cottages of Shorwell are remarkable for their neatness and comfortable appearance, as well as for the abundant display of creepers and flowering shrubs with which most of them are adorned.

Two miles further on we enter BRIXTON, a populous village in the heart of a rich tract of cultivation: is one mile from the shore, and screened from the north by a range of lofty downs. The Church is rather spacious, and not unpicturesque; many of the cottages are neat, some few furnished for lodgings: and there is a comfortable small inn. This place is commonly called Brison, and one clergyman names it Brightstone.

MOTTISTONE succeeds: a pretty hamlet nearly shrouded in wood, with a very picturesque church. On an elevated part of the farm are the remains of some small druidical temple called LONGSTONE, which is a rude piece of rock of a quadrangular figure, evidently erected by art, and rears itself about twelve feet above the ground; near it another large stone lies partly buried in the earth, of not less than eight feet long.

BROOK is the last village we pass till we reach Freshwater: much the same character as the others: the Mansion-house, which is surrounded with wood, being the only object to notice, besides the little church, which we shall presently pass, posted solitarily on an eminence near the foot of the down.

CHAPTER IV.

THE WESTERN QUARTER OF THE ISLAND, DISTINGUISHED

FOR ITS

SUBLIME SCENERY.

*The Road over the Downs from Brooke to Freshwater-gate.*

We shall now leave the familiar scenes of cultivation and of village life for a time, to enjoy the charms of unbounded prospect, as we journey for four miles over a succession of pasturing downs, where in many parts our road will be upon a natural carpet of the finest turf.

Tasteless indeed must be those who can travel over these lofty and *beautiful* downs, without experiencing the most lively gratification from the chequered and magnificent prospects which invite their contemplation on every side: but to enjoy the pleasure in perfection we must occasionally pause, to discriminate (by reference to a friend or a map,) some of the more remarkable features.—Looking to the westward, the high cliffs of Freshwater stretch away in a noble promontory of three miles, forming the foreground to the soft azure perspective of the coast of Dorset: but to the north, so diversified is the extensive landscape with towns and villages, hills, woods, forests, sea, and river, as to mock our most ardent wishes to convey even a faint idea of the grandeur of the composition.

Another source of no inconsiderable pleasure, when traversing these beautiful downs,—soaring as it were in the higher regions—is feeling that we actually breathe the purest atmosphere, so exhilarating to the human frame. Nor is the reverse of this desirable clearness of the weather without its share of amusement—to witness the formation of clouds, as the vapors are drawn up from the sea, and gradually condensed; rolling by, and enveloping us in their

103

misty volumes. It is true indeed, that these exhibitions are not without danger to the traveller, lest he unwarily approach too near the fatal precipice: but this circumstance imposing the necessity of caution, excites an *interest*—and interest is the very zest of adventure. [Footnote: Near the edge of the cliffs about half a mile eastward of Freshwater-gate, a small tablet has lately been erected, to commemorate the unfortunate fate of a youth who slipped over and perished on the rocks beneath.—Some years ago two successive keepers of the Needles Light-house lost their lives in a similar manner over the precipices on which that establishment is located.]

In short, whether for the splendor of the prospects, the refreshing purity of the air, or the novelty of literally walking in the clouds, we esteem the journey over these downs, as pleasurable as any portion of the tour.

We shall now suppose the Visitor to be descending the last down, and in a few minutes, walking on the beach—here to commence his examination of ...

### THE FRESHWATER CLIFFS.

FRESHWATER BAY, I.W. (*The two remarkable isolated Rocks and Entrance to the principal Cavern.*)

"Suspended cliffs, with hideous sway,
Seem nodding o'er the caverns gray."

☞ *Several romantic* CAVERNS *near Freshwater-gate: the Needles* LIGHT-
HOUSE—*and the wonderfully* COLORED SANDS *of Alum Bay, are accessible
without taking boat: the celebrated* NEEDLE ROCKS *are seen (though not to
advantage,) from the down and beach: but the* GRAND ARCH, *the* WEDGE-
ROCK, *and several deep* CAVERNS *and other curiosities of Rock-scenery,
can be viewed only by water, which is extremely desirable in calm weather.*

---

THE WHITE CLIFFS OF ALBION is so favorite a poetical designation of
the English coast, that it is with some degree of pride we hail our
"sea-girt isle" as surpassing in the magnificence and splendor of this
characteristic, every other part of the kingdom; for even
Shakspeare's cliff at Dover, immortalized as it is by the pen of the
bard himself, is little more than half the elevation of some of the
chalk precipices of the Isle of Wight,—which, at Freshwater, rise
from the bosom of the blue ocean with a perpendicular face of the
most dazzling whiteness, the sublime altitude of more than 600
feet!—being nearly one-half higher than the pinnacles either of St.
Paul's or Salisbury Cathedrals.

A stranger from the inland districts, who may never have seen a
precipice upon a grander scale than is presented by the sides of some
deep chalk-pit, would be at a loss to imagine wherein consisted the
BEAUTY and the INTEREST of such seemingly monotonous scenes;
especially when informed that they are indebted to no borrowed
ornament from either tree or shrub: and indeed it would prove
equally difficult on our part to furnish a comprehensive definition.
One eminent writer enthusiastically eulogises their appearance as
"*singularly elegant* when viewed at a proper distance; and with the
Needle Rocks, constituting a whole that is scarcely to be equalled:"—
another declares that "the most lofty and magnificent fabrics of Art,
compared with these stupendous works of Nature, sink in idea to
Lilliputian size:"—and a third, that "the towering precipices of

Scratchell's Bay are of the most elegant forms;" and "the pearly hue of the chalk is beyond description by words, probably out of the power even of the pencil."

------

As almost every visitor has a card of *all the local curiosities* presented to him by some of the boatmen of the place, it would be useless here to describe individually the several objects deserving personal observation: we shall therefore confine our notice to a few of the most prominent, — commencing at ...

## FRESHWATER-GATE,

Remarkable for the brilliancy as well as beauty of the surrounding promontories, of which an enchanting view is presented as we descend from the downs. The outline of the precipices is here extremely bold, forming several charming little coves or bays, and penetrated at the base by numerous deep CAVERNS of the most romantic formation, that are exceedingly interesting to visitors when explored. But what contributes most to the picturesque character of the scenery is the presence of several immense isolated rocks of grotesque shape, that rise from 30 to 60 feet above the sea. Two of these will particularly attract attention, namely, the *Arched*, and the *Deer-pound*, [Footnote: This name was given to the rock from the fact, it is said, of a deer having leaped on it from the main land, when closely pursued by the hounds of the late Lord Holmes, about 70 or 80 years ago: at which time the separation could have been but a few yards! Whatever credit may be attached to this anecdote by the reader, it at least serves to show the opinion which the older inhabitants entertain of the progressive waste of land at this part of the coast (the face of the cliffs being constantly exposed to the weather and undermining action of the sea); and we remember it was but a few years back when the top of this same rock was covered with a considerable patch of green sod.] they are the remains of the original cliff, but being composed of more stubborn and adhesive materials, have long resisted the lashing waves and warring elements, while the parent cliffs are constantly receding and forming a wider separation.

Here are two respectable Hotels: the *Albion*, close to the beach; and *Plumbly's*, on the cliff: both of which offer to their guests the charm of hearing ...

> — —"The restless waves that roar,
> And fling their foam against the rocky shore."

The CAVERN in Freshwater Bay was formerly an object of no little curiosity to those who had never seen any thing similar of a more striking character; but the romantic effect, and consequently interest of the scene has been greatly injured by the fall falling-in of the arched roof. Now, however, visitors can easily investigate other caverns of a similar nature at WATCOMBE BAY (to which a good road has been made from Plumbly's Hotel,) where there is also a pyramidical rock, curiously perforated at the base.

A very common way of seeing these precipices is to go by water to Alum Bay, there land, walk up to the Light-house, and return by the beacon: or take boat at Alum Bay, and sail round the Needles or to Freshwater Bay, just as fancy may suggest. Some proceed on foot from Freshwater-gate to the Needles Light-house (about three miles), on the green sod, near the margin of the cliffs: other parties again go round by the carriage-road the whole distance in their vehicles. As, however, the grandest scenes can only be visited by boat, we shall best perform our duty as Cicerone by pointing them out as they appear in an aquatic excursion—that to parties generally affords a degree of elevated pleasure to which nothing else in the island can bear any comparison. Yet should the weather be too rough for this to be enjoyed, the visit to Freshwater may prove not the less interesting: since it is impossible for any spectacle to exceed in sublimity that which is displayed when a storm is raging around the majestic cliffs and vast detached rocks that here encounter the winds and waves of the British Channel:—

"Down bursts the gale—the surges sweep,
Like gathering hosts, against the steep,
Sheeting, with clouds of snowy spray,
Its lofty forehead, old and gray.
With sudden shriek and cowering wing,
To the wild cliff the sea-birds spring;
Careering o'er the darken'd heaven,
The clouds in warring heaps are driven;
And crested high with lawny foam,
Rushes the mighty billow home."

(Another Hotel is situated on the north side of the down, within sight of the Needles, by whose name it is distinguished.)

WATCOMBE BAY *FRESHWATER ISLE OF WIGHT.*

From Watcombe Bay the precipices continue to increase in height till they reach their greatest elevation (617 feet) at HIGH-DOWN, on which the beacon is erected: they are however less perpendicular here than we shall presently find them; and the more sloping portions are covered by extensive patches of turf, samphire, &c., which vary the pure white of the upright masses, though perhaps the lofty appearance of the whole is thereby rather diminished, at least to a spectator at their base. Amongst the most remarkable objects in this part of the range are NEPTUNE'S CAVE, and LORD HOLMES'S PARLOUR:—the latter, a cavern of considerable height and breadth, derives its name from the nobleman, whose name it bears, having occasionally enjoyed a repast with his friends in the briny coolness of its shade, at least so tradition tells us: it can be easily entered by boat in calm weather: and when viewed from beneath its rough vaulted roof, has certainly a very romantic appearance.

A little further on is the WEDGE-ROCK, a most singular result of accident; being a piece of rock about twelve feet long by six or eight wide, exactly the shape of a wedge, resting between the main cliff and a large mass of detached chalk, just as if fixed there by some gigantic hand to effect the separation. It is often practicable to land here, and it is worth while on the part of the young and active, were it only to be satisfied how extremely deceptive is the appearance of the rocks and broken green ledges, as to their size and extent of surface,—for few would suppose (in passing by,) that the piece near the Wedge-rock contains upwards of an acre of ground.—The pyramidical mass connected with the Wedge is about fifty feet high, and a hundred long at the base.

Our friends will remember (as has been before said,) that we leave the history of many curious rocks and caverns to be given by the local watermen; for personal examination will invest a scene or object with a degree of interest which cannot be felt by the reader, who may have no expectation of ever seeing them.

Passing the OLD PEPPER-ROCK, a picturesque detached mass at the foot of the chalk—we find ourselves under the noble promontory of MAIN-BENCH, where the precipices again rise to upwards, of six hundred feet in height: and being nearly perpendicular, present a truly sublime aspect, viewed either from above or below: while the constant washing of the waves at the lower part, by removing the looser particles of chalk, gives it much the appearance of having been built with vast blocks of masonry. As the water is deep even close to the cliff, and beautifully transparent in calm weather, the reflection on its surface of the crags above, and the sunken rocks and marine plants which appear beneath, must add considerably to the interest of our aquatic excursion. Main-bench terminates in a bold bluff or projecting angle called SUN CORNER; rounding which, we enter ...

SCRATCHELL'S BAY, universally considered by visitors as the most memorable spot on the island coast, alike for the grandeur, beauty, and variety of its scenery. The dazzling whiteness of the chalk is here relieved by thin curving beds of dark flint, which regularly divide it into parallel strata of eight or ten feet thickness; the towering precipices are of the most picturesque shapes; and the Needle Rocks form an inimitable termination to the scene. Just within the bay is the NEEDLES CAVE, the deepest along the whole range, as it penetrates the chalk 300 feet: but the *unique* feature which above all the rest claims attention is the niche-like recess in the face of the cliff, appropriately designated ...

THE GRAND ARCH;

It indicates little that is remarkable at a distance; but a truly sublime effect is produced when the stranger is placed under its awful roof with his back against the concave chalk: for he then sees above him a magnificent Arch two hundred feet in height and overhanging the beach at least one hundred and eighty!—yet so true, nay, even elegant is the sweep, that it rather resembles the stupendous work of Art, than the casual production of Nature. To form an idea of the sublimity of the scene, the reader should task his memory with the dimensions of some of the proudest architectural monuments in Great Britain: and the comparison would immediately remove all doubt, that a sight of the Arch itself would amply repay the trouble of a visit to Freshwater.

SCRATCHELL'S BAY, *And the NEEDLE ROCKS, as viewed from a bold Bluff called Sun Corner, being the termination of the Freshwater Cliffs.— Isle if Wight.*

Scratchell's Bay is about half-a-mile in breadth; being formed by Sun Corner and the Grand Arch on the eastern side, and on the west by the

## NEEDLE ROCKS,

Which stretch out into the sea a considerable distance: they are remains of the original cliff, and forcibly illustrate the destructive power of the ocean's stormy winds and waves, which in successive ages have removed so vast a quantity of the adjacent chalk. Nor are their ravages at all diminished at the present time: for it is only within the last few years that the smallest rock has been completely insulated; while another immense mass of the cliff is evidently separating by degrees, and will probably become ere long entirely detached, forming a magnificent pyramid two or three hundred feet high. It is impossible to convey by verbal description a correct idea of these celebrated rocks: for in passing round or through them, they assume a different shape almost every dozen yards; sometimes appearing like a continuation of the main promontory,—sometimes as one or more lofty acuminated pyramids,—or again we see the different masses extending in nearly a straight line, between which we catch a distant view of Christchurch and other objects on the opposite coast. The name (inappropriate to their present form,) was derived from a spiry rock, 120 feet high and very slender, which fell in the year 1764, having been nearly worn through by the incessant action of the tides: its base however is still visible at low water.

The *Pomone,* a fifty-gun frigate, was wrecked on the most western of these rocks, on June 11th, 1811, when returning home after an absence of three years; but owing to the fineness of the weather, the crew and passengers, including some Persian princes, reached the shore in safety; and most of her guns and stores were removed before she went to pieces. "The vessel," says Mr. Webster, "afforded me a scale by which to judge of the size of the Needles, and I was surprized to find that the hull of the frigate did not reach one-fourth of their height." The entrance to the Solent Channel "through the Needles" was always considered hazardous for ships of great burthen, not only on account of those rocks, but also of the immense banks of pebbles or "Shingles" that lie to the westward: recent surveys have however ascertained that the channel has sufficient width and depth for the safe passage of the largest ships of war.

### ALUM BAY.

The brilliant and novel display of rock scenery which this spot affords, and its being easily accessible either by water or land (for a road leads to it from the north side of the down), cause it to be universally visited by strangers who extend their tour to this quarter of the island. It is bounded on the south by the Needles and the snowy precipices of which they once formed part: but its greatest celebrity is owing to the wonderful diversity and brightness in the cliffs on the opposite side, which are composed of sand, clay, and ochreous earths, disposed in alternate *vertical* strata: and as the torrents of winter carry away vast masses of the soil, forming numerous deep ravines—an endless variety of the most beautiful peaks and romantic forms are thus produced. The colored strata vary in thickness from a sheet of paper to several yards; are now purely white, black, red, or yellow; then brown, blueish, or dull green,—alternating in a surprizing manner with each other, or blending into every hue: and many of the tints so vivid, yet so delicate, that they are justly compared to the variegations of a tulip, or to the shades of silk. "Alum Bay," says an eminent geologist, "is so extraordinary a place, that I am unable to explain in adequate terms, the surprize I felt on first seeing it. The scenery is indeed of a species unique in this country: and nothing that I had previously seen bore the least resemblance to it." This spot owes its name to the fact of alum having been occasionally found on its shores.

And now, having pointed out the most remarkable features in the cliffs, it only remains to notice THE LIGHT-HOUSE, which is a gratifying object of curiosity to persons unacquainted with the nature of such an establishment, it stands near the extremity of the down, and commands a prospect of great extent and beauty, particularly of the unrivaled scenery of Alum Bay. The Needles are seen to most advantage from the water: but when this has not been enjoyed, the party should cautiously approach within a few yards of the precipice, "and to those whose nerves are proof against the horrors of the position, the new into the bays beneath, and of the cliffs and Needle Rocks, is extremely sublime. The agitation and sound of the waves below are hardly perceived, and it is scarcely possible to imagine that the quiet expanse which now seems stretched in boundless repose under the eye, is the same turbulent element which had but lately been seen bursting in clouds of foam, and thundering on its rocky shore.—In hard blowing weather, the fury of the wind on this promontory is scarcely credible. Very large flints and fragments of chalk are blown from the cliffs, so as to endanger the windows of the light-house; and for many days in succession, it is scarcely possible to open the door."

The precipices of Freshwater, like those at Bembridge, are frequented at periodical seasons by prodigious flights of sea-fowl of various kinds. The birds are taken by the country-people at the hazard of their lives; they descend by means of a stout rope which turns round a crow-bar firmly fixed in the ground above; one end of the rope being fastened about their body, and the other end held in their hands, by which they lower and raise themselves from ledge to ledge of the horrid precipice. The aquatic fowl furnish most amusing sport to numberless shooting-parties during the season. The principal species are ... puffins, gulls, cormorants, Cornish choughs, the eider duck, auks, divers, guillemots, razor-bills, widgeons, willocks, daws, starlings, and pigeons. Their breeding-season is in the months of May, June, and July, and towards the end of August the greater part of them migrate with their new generations. Their flesh is too rank and fishy to be eaten, and is used only for baiting crab and lobster pots; the feathers are valuable, and the eggs are bought chiefly by visitors for curiosity.

## THE ROADS TO YARMOUTH, NEWPORT, &c.

☞ *Having visited the western extremity of the Island, we return — either by* CALBOURNE *to Newport, which is the nearest; or round by* YARMOUTH, *this being perhaps the less monotonous road of the two.*

The tourist, on leaving the magnificent scenes of the western coast, can hardly expect to see many spots in the remainder of his journey, capable of engaging his attention. He may still however enjoy some very charming prospects, particularly in the neighbourhood of Yarmouth, whither we shall now suppose him to shape his course.

We shall pass two seats: FARRINGFORD, on the north side of the down, surrounded by flourishing plantations; and about a mile and a half further, the fine old manor-house of AFTON.

THE VILLAGE OF FRESHWATER is prettily interspersed with wood; but except the church (whose front is more picturesque than most in the island), has nothing to notice;—unless it should fortunately happen to be high-tide at the time of our passing, and then the RIVER YAR will have a lovely effect—winding between gently rising banks feathered with grove and copse, shrouding here a mansion, and there a cottage; while pleasure-boats and an unusual number of swans are seen gliding and sporting on its silver bosom.

Passing over a neat bridge, and through the fertile parish of THORLEY, whose church is the plainest in the island, we reach

## YARMOUTH,

Standing opposite Lymington, and once a place of considerable importance, having obtained a charter of franchises in the reign of Henry II: it is very clean and open,—and being situated in the neighbourhood of the most interesting coast scenery, is upon the whole an agreeable place, particularly for gentlemen partial to marine pleasures. Its chief support is derived from the shipping that anchor in its excellent roadsted, and the passengers to and from Lymington; there are three inns—the principal one (the George,) is a large ancient building, formerly the Governor's house, where King Charles II was entertained by Sir Rt. Holmes on his paying the island a visit in 1667.—The Church has recently received the ornament of a new tower, and the interior boasts a good statue of the above-named Sir Robert. The Castle (as it is called), is a heavy, plain mass of building, constructed in the reign of Henry VIII to protect this entrance to the Solent Channel.

The village of NORTON is on the opposite side of the river, where there are several very respectable villas,—so sheltered by groves and

Brannon's Picture of the Isle of Wight

shrubberies, that the whole neighbourhood presents the delightful appearance of a bold foreland completely shrouded in wood, even to the water's edge.

Opposite *Carey's Sconce*, half a mile west of Norton, is HURST CASTLE, built at the extremity of a long strip of shingly land stretching out from the Hampshire coast, which here contracts the width of the Solent Channel to less than a mile. Close by are two Light-houses, erected for the purpose of assisting ships to clear the passage through the Needles.

Four miles from Yarmouth we pass through SHALFLEET, a clean and populous village: the Church is next the road, of a heavy construction,—yet affording a good subject for a sketch. Northward is NEWTOWN, a very ancient borough; which was a populous place in the time of Richard II (when it was burned by the French, but soon afterwards rebuilt), and though now reduced to a few humble cottages, the course of its streets may yet be traced. It has a new church, of a neat design; and is noted for its extensive salterns, and convenient haven.—Previously to the passing of the Reform Bill in 1832, Yarmouth and Newtown each returned two members to parliament.

*The Road by Calbourne and Carisbrooke.*

The direct road from Freshwater-gate to Newport runs for the first three or four miles at the northern foot of the range of downs described at p. 89; presenting no object worthy of separate remark till we reach CALBOURNE, a considerable village, having a decent small inn. The pretty situation of its neat little Church and Parsonage,—the handsome mansion and luxuriant plantations of a first-rate seat called WESTOVER, close by,—with a small stream running through the grounds and in front of the neighbouring cottages,—altogether produce a very pleasing scene ...

"Where sweet simplicity resides, which Grace
And Beauty call their own."

Two miles further we pass SWAINSTON, another principal seat: the mansion lies below the road, surrounded by trees; a copious stream, well stored with fish, runs through the gardens and plantations, which are extensive and judiciously laid-out; and the prospect-temple which crowns the hill on the right is a very conspicuous object. From hence the road is on the slope of a series of hills, often picturesquely shrouded in groves and hanging woods; while in the more open parts some extensive views are presented of the north side of the island, the sea, and the opposite coast of Hampshire; but the prospect which is opened as we descend into Carisbrooke is particularly grand: the village makes an admirable foreground, backed by lofty hills, —on the left we see the town of Newport and its adjoining hamlets, with E. Cowes Park, &c. in the distance, —and on the right,

"High o'er the pines, that with their dark'ning shade
    Surround yon craggy bank, THE CASTLE rears
Its crumbling turrets: still its towering head
    A warlike mien, a sullen grandeur wears!"

## LANDMARKS AND OTHER CONSPICUOUS OBJECTS

*Erected on the Hills.*

The fact of so many of the hills and downs being crowned with some far-seen object, such as a light-house, obelisk, or telegraph, must be a source of considerable interest to a traveller in the Isle of Wight, not only by their often giving an identity and attraction to many of those broad features of scenery which would otherwise be comparatively tame and monotonous, but also by enabling him to determine the bearings and situation of places in their vicinity.

We shall here name a few of the most conspicuous of these objects, nearly in the order pursued in the preceding description of the Tour of the Island:—most of them being visible from the neighbourhood of Newport, which, as we have before stated, occupies a central position. We shall therefore commence with Carisbrooke Castle.

At West Cowes—the Church-tower, and Windmills. At East Cowes—Towers of Osborne, Norris, and East Cowes Castle. At Wootton—the Prospect-tower of Fernhill. Southward of Ryde—a large Windmill. On Ashey Down—the Sea-mark. At Bembridge—Mill on the Down. Godshill—the Church: behind which, on Appuldurcombe Down, is an Obelisk and private Signal-station. On Shanklin Down—Cooke's Castle. St. Catharine's Down—ancient Tower, and old Light-house; on the sea-cliffs, the new Light-house; on the northern extremity of the down, the Alexandrian Pillar. Freshwater Downs—Light-house, and Beacon.

## TOURS OF THE ISLAND.

Some years ago it was customary for the then limited number of Post-masters to adopt a regular three-days' Tour of the island, dividing it into the North-eastern, the Southern, and the North-western; differing but very little except as to the *order* of the days' excursion. Not so now—for a hundred plans would hardly describe all "the Tours" recommended by the different inn-keepers and numerous other letters-out of vehicles for pleasure-parties; to say nothing of the wide difference between the visitors themselves, as regards the *Time* allowed.—We have anticipated, we hope, every question on the subject, by the arrangement in the preceding pages: but still it may be satisfactory to some of our readers, to see the most generally adopted Routes. The reader will perceive that *Appuldurcombe* is frequently left as the object of a separate day's trip.

## CONTINUED TOUR FROM RYDE.

**FIRST DAY**

| | MILES. |
|---|---|
| St. John's: St. Clare, &c., | 1 |
| The Priory, | 2 |
| St. Helen's Green, | 1 |
| Bembridge (crossing ferry), | 1 |
| Yaverland, | 3½ |
| Sandown Fort and Village, | 1½ |
| Shanklin Chine and Village, | 3 |
| Luccombe Chine, | 1½ |
| East End, | 0½ |
| Bonchurch—Ventnor, | 2 |
| Steephill Castle, | 1 |
| St. Lawrence, | 1 |
| Niton, | 2½ |
| Sleep here, or at Blackgang. | —— |
| | 23½ |

**SECOND DAY**

| | |
|---|---|
| St. Catharine's Light-house, | 0½ |
| Sandrock Spring, | 0½ |
| Blackgang Chine, | 0½ |
| Chale, | 0½ |
| Kingston, | 2½ |
| Shorwell and Northcourt, | 2 |

*(Second day continued.)*

| | MILES. |
|---|---|
| Brixton, | 2 |
| Mottistone, | 2 |
| Brooke, | 1 |
| Freshwater-gate, | 4 |
| Needles Light-house, | 3½ |
| Alum Bay, | 1 |
| Sleep at Fr. gate or A. Bay. | —— |
| | 20 |

**THIRD DAY**

| | |
|---|---|
| Yarmouth, | 6 |
| Calbourne and Westover, | 6 |
| Swainston, | 1½ |
| Carisbrooke Village, | 3 |
| Newport, | 1 |
| Parkhurst Prison, | 1 |
| West Cowes, | 4 |
| East Cowes (crossing ferry), | 0½ |
| Whippingham Church, | 2 |
| Wootton-bridge, | 3 |
| Quarr Abbey, | 1 |
| Ryde, | 2½ |
| | —— |
| | 31½ |

*Tour from Ryde, in which Parties sleep but one Night in the Country.*

FIRST DAY: St. Helen's 4 miles, Bembridge 1, Yaverland and Sandown 5, Shanklin 3, Luccombe and East End 2, Bonchurch and Ventnor 2, Wroxall 2, Newchurch 4, Ryde 6—total 29 miles, or by Brading 26.

SECOND DAY: Wootton 3½, Arreton 4, Godshill and Appuldurcombe 5, Steephill 3, St. Lawrence 1, Niton 2½, Arreton 7, Wootton 4, Ryde 3½—total 33½ miles.

THIRD DAY: Through Wootton to Newport 7, Carisbrooke 1, Shorwell 4, Brixton 2, Mottistone 2, Brooke 1, Freshwater-gate 4, Needles-point 3½, Alum Bay 1,—total 25½ miles. Sleep at Fr. gate or Alum Bay.—FOURTH DAY: Yarmouth 6, Shalfleet 4, Barracks, &c. 5½, West Cowes, 4, East Cowes 0½, Whippingham 2, Wootton 3, Ryde 3½—total 28½ miles.

## GENERAL TOUR FROM COWES.

| FIRST DAY | | *(Second day continued.)* | |
|---|---|---|---|
| House of Industry, &c. | 4 | Steephill Castle, | 1 |
| Newport, | 1 | Ventnor, and Bonchurch, | 2 |
| Carisbrooke Castle, | 1 | East End, | 1 |
| Swainston, on the right, | 3 | Luccombe Chine, | 0½ |
| Calbourne and Westover, | 1½ | Shanklin Chine and Village, | 1½ |
| Yarmouth, | 6 | Sleep here, or at Ventnor | — — |
| Alum Bay, | 6 | | 24 |
| The Needles Light-house, | 1 | THIRD DAY | |
| Freshwater-gate, | 3½ | Sandown Fort and Village, | 3 |
| Sleep here, or at Alum Bay. | — — | Yaverland Church, &c. | 1½ |
| | 28 | Bembridge.—Cross ferry, | 3½ |
| SECOND DAY | | St. Helen's Green, | 1 |
| Brooke—Mottistone, | 5 | The Priory, on the right, | 1 |

| | | | |
|---|---|---|---|
| Brixton, | 2 | St. Clare—St. John's, | 2 |
| Shorwell and Northcourt, | 2 | Ryde, | 1 |
| Chale and Blackgang Chine, | 5 | Wootton-bridge—Fernhill, | 3½ |
| Sandrock Spring, | 0½ | Whippingham Church, | 3 |
| St. Catharine's Light-house, | 0½ | East Cowes, | 2 |
| Niton Village, | 0½ | | —— |
| St. Lawrence Church, &c. | 2½ | | 21½ |

## TOURS FROM NEWPORT.

### NORTH-EASTERN TOUR

| | | | |
|---|---|---|---|
| Fernhill—Wootton-bridge, | 3½ | Yaverland Church, &c. | 3½ |
| Quarr Abbey, | 1½ | Sandown Fort and Village, | 1½ |
| Ryde, | 2 | Brading Down, | 3 |
| St. John's—St. Clare, | 1 | Ashey Sea-mark, | 2 |
| The Priory, | 2 | Down-end, | 2 |
| St. Helen's Green, | 1 | Newport, | 3 |
| Cross ferry to Bembridge, | 1 | | —— |
| | | | 27 |

SOUTHERN TOUR.

WESTERN TOUR.

| | | | |
|---|---|---|---|
| Arreton Church, | 4 | Carisbrooke, | 1 |
| Shanklin, | 6 | Shorwell and Northcourt, | 4 |
| Luccombe—East End, | 2 | Brixton, | 2 |
| Bonchurch and Ventnor, | 2 | Mottistone, | 2 |
| Steephill Castle, | 1 | Brooke, | 1 |
| St. Lawrence, | 1 | Freshwater-gate, | 4 |
| Niton, | 2½ | Needles Light-house, | 3½ |
| St. Catharine's Light-house, | 0½ | Alum Bay, | 1 |
| Sandrock Spring, | 0½ | Yarmouth, | 6 |
| Blackgang Chine, | 0½ | Calbourne and Westover, | 6 |
| Chale, | 1 | Swainston, | 1½ |
| Gatcombe, | 4½ | Carisbrooke Village, | 3 |
| Newport, | 4 | Newport, | 1 |
| (Or return by Rookley.) | —— | (Or return by Shalfleet.) | —— |
| | 29 | | 36 |

## A VOYAGE ROUND THE ISLAND

If the weather be favorable, will prove very interesting, and indeed be necessary to enable us to form a just estimate of the local attractions, since many of the scenes we have described are seen to most advantage from the water. Steamers perform the trip two or three times a-week during the season (usually in about eight hours): and sailing-craft from Ryde and Cowes are often engaged by parties for the same purpose.

If we sail to the eastward on leaving Cowes Harbour, the first objects demanding our attention are Norris Castle and the royal Palace of Osborne, with their extensive lawns sweeping to the shore, shaded by numerous groups of noble trees. After passing the Creeks of King's Quay and Wootton, we have a partial sight of Binstead: and a most comprehensive view of the fashionable town of Ryde, just as we leave the Pier. Hence to St. Helen's the coast forms several beautiful bays, lined with gentlemen's seats and villas, hamlets, and luxuriant woods.

Brading Haven, with the adjacent villages of Bembridge, St. Helen's, and Brading,—the whole encompassed by a semi-circular range of lofty hills—forms a very agreeable picture, especially at the time of high water. Our readers will have no difficulty in recognising the landmark of St. Helen's tower on the beach, and that on Ashey Down, about four miles inland.

Two miles further are the lofty Culver Cliffs, forming the north side of Sandown Bay, on whose shores stand the village and fort of the same name. At the southern extremity of this extensive bay rise the dark precipices of Dunnose, penetrated by the Chines of Shanklin and Luccombe. Near the latter commences the celebrated tract called the Undercliff, whose varied and unique charms are nowhere so advantageously seen as from the water, "whence it rises like a series of gigantic steps that seem to lead from the lofty cliffs on the shore, to the summit of the grand perpendicular wall" that bounds it on the land-side.—East End, the lovely village of Bonchurch, the fast-increasing town of Ventnor, and the stately castle of Steephill, are all fully presented to our view: and less distinctly through the groves in which they are for the most part embosomed, the villas of St. Lawrence, Old Park, Mirables, &c. Beyond the pretty little cove of Puckaster we see part of Niton village; and close to the shore, the gigantic tower of the Light-house. A mile further is the Sandrock Spring, in the midst of a wild tract, that terminates in the gloomy ravine called Blackgang Chine, backed by the tower-crowned eminence of St. Catharine's Hill.

Hence to Compton Bay the coast is dreary and comparatively monotonous; but we have a tolerable view of some of the smaller chines, and also of the fine range of downs that stretch from the centre of the island to its western extremity. Almost the whole extent of Freshwater Cliffs meets the eye at once: but there is no great difficulty in recognizing the most noted rocks, caves, &c. as we pass along. The various forms which are exhibited by those huge masses of chalk the Needles, as we approach and leave them, in connection with the beautiful precipices of Scratchell's Bay, form perhaps the most interesting circumstance of our voyage: the light-house seems placed on the very brink of the precipice: and the brilliant scenery of Alum Bay will appear to advantage, especially if it be a sunny afternoon.

Beyond this the coast consists of steep broken slopes and earthy cliffs, some of them of considerable altitude, but presents no object of particular interest till we near the river Yar, with its adjacent town and villas: Newtown Creek opens about three miles further on. West Cowes, as we approach it from Thorness Bay, has a beautiful aspect, numerous genteel villas and first-rate lodging-houses covering the shore for nearly a mile: and the ever-amusing scene of Cowes harbour will form a delightful termination to our voyage.

The Passage and Conveyance.

JUNE 1, 1849.

## BY STEAM-PACKETS.

☞ *Strangers are particularly requested to attend to the following recommendation.*—We have always made it a point to delay the publication of our Guides to as late a period as we well could (often to a degree of inconvenience), in order that our readers may be furnished with an accurate statement of the precise time of the several passage-vessels starting to or from the island: but this, instead of an advantage, often proved a disappointment: for perhaps a change of hours unexpectedly took place within a week or fortnight afterwards, in consequence of some new regulation in the time of the railways, or from some motive on the part of one or other of the steam-packet companies. We therefore particularly advise strangers to make inquiry at the local inns, on board the packets, or at the railway or booking offices, in all cases where it is of important consequence to know exactly to a minute.

*Between Southampton, Cowes, Ryde, & Portsmouth.*

| FROM | MORN. | AFT. |
|---|---|---|
| South'n to Cowes at. | 3½ 8.40 10.40— | 1¾ 4.40 7 |
| Ryde and Portsmo. | 8.40 10.40— | 1¾ 4.40 |
| Portsmouth to Cowes | 8.40 10— | 2 4½ 6½ |
| Southampton | 8.40 10— | 2 4½ |

| | | |
|---|---|---|
| Ryde to Cowes | 9¼  10½ — | 2½  5  7 |
| Southampton | 9¼  10½ — | 2½  5 |
| Cowes to Ryde | 10  12 — | 3½  6¼ |
| Portsmouth | 6¾  10  12 — | 3½  6.15 |
| South'n. | 8¾  10.40  12 — | 3¾  6¼  8¾ |
| South'n to East Cowes | 3½  10.40 — | 1¾  4.40 |
| E. Cowes to South'ton. | 8.35  11.50 — | 3.35  6 |

On Sundays the passages are less frequent.

---

*Portsmouth, Portsea, Gosport, and Ryde.*

From Gosport at 8.10, 9.45, 10.50, 11.50, 1½, 2½, 5¼, 6.35. From Portsea at 8.15, 9.50, 10.55 11.55, 1.35, 2.35, 5.25, 6.40. From Portsmouth each passage five minutes later.

From Ryde at 7.20, 9, 11, 12, 1¼, 2½, 4¼, & 6.

ON SUNDAYS:

From Portsmouth at 8, 3, and 5.
From Ryde at 9, 4, and 6.

☞ *In the height of the season, steamers leave Southampton for Cowes on the arrival of every Railway train, — and Cowes for Southampton in time to meet every Train: and between Portsmouth and Ryde run about every hour from 7 to 7.*

---

From LYMINGTON — the *Glasgow* runs to Yarmouth three or four times a-day: the *Solent* every morning to Cowes, whence she proceeds on alternate days to Southampton and Portsmouth — and by suiting her time to that of the other steamers, maintains a daily communication between all these places.

The steamers from Portsmouth, Southampton, and Lymington, tow horse-boats across.

During summer, Steamers frequently make trips round the island, usually in about seven hours.

*Regular Sailing Passage-boats.*

FROM COWES to NEWPORT, daily: the hours depending upon the state of the tide.

From WOOTTON to PORTSMOUTH at 9 and 4 (3 or earlier in winter), daily: and from Portsmouth at 9 and 2½.

From BEMBRIDGE to Portsmouth and back, every other day, or oftener, in summer.

To POOLE the sailing-hoys run twice a-week, calling off Cowes and Yarmouth.

Land-Conveyances.

The STAGE-COACHES.—The following are the summer arrangements for 1849:—

From Newport to Ryde, at 8, 12½, 2¾, and 5¼. From Ryde at 9¼, 11, 3½, and 6½.

From Newport to West Cowes at 8, 9½, 2½, and 5½. Cowes to Newport at 10, 12, 3½, and 6½.

West Cowes to Ventnor (thro' Newport, Blackgang, and Niton,) at 10, returning at 3. Ventnor to East Cowes (through Godshill and Newport,) at 8½, returning at 3.

From Ryde to Ventnor at 9½, 11, and 3. Ventnor to Ryde at 8½, 1¾, and 3. Passing through Brading, Sandown, and Shanklin.

Most of the coaches omit travelling on Sundays.

It will be seen that by these conveyances, visitors arriving at Cowes or Ryde in the morning may make the tour of one-half the island the same day. If from Ryde in the morning, they would be returned to Cowes in time for the last packet across, and the same from the latter to the former place.

But here we must caution our friends, as we did respecting the steam-packets, that frequent alterations take place in the hours of starting, perhaps in consequence of some change made by the vessels, but as often induced by the caprice of the rival speculators; some of them continuing throughout the year, and others running only during the summer.

The CARRIERS.—These of late have so increased, that there is scarcely a village without one or more to Newport or Ryde,—between the latter places there are three every day; between Cowes, Newport, and Ventnor, several carts and vans daily; and from the less populous parishes, one every other day.

List of the Principal Inns.

| | |
|---|---|
| NEWPORT, — | the Bugle—Mew. |
| | Star—Bryant. |
| | Wheat-sheaf, Corn-market—J. Read. |
| | Green Dragon, Pyle-street—R. Read. |
| | Swan, High-street—Wardle. |
| RYDE, — | Pier Hotel—Rendall. |
| | Hotel, Union-street—Yelf. |
| | Kent, ditto—Pegg. |
| | Crown, near the theatre—Woodrow. |
| | Hotel, near the pier—Beazley. |
| | Star, upper part of the town—Locke. |
| | Hotel & Boarding-house—Weeks. |
| SPRING-VALE, — | Tavern—Heath. |
| WEST COWES, — — | Fountain, on the quay—Webb. |
| | Vine, adjoining; ditto—Roper. |
| | Marine Hotel, Parade—Helmore. |
| | Globe, ditto—Aris. |
| EAST COWES, — | Medina Hotel—Drew. |
| | Prince of Wales, nr. toll-gate—Tucker. |
| YARMOUTH, — | George—Bright. |
| | Bugle—Butler. |
| FRESHWATER, — | Hotel. Fr. gate—Plumbly. |
| | Albion Hotel, ditto—Groves. |
| | Needles Hotel, Alum Bay—Groves. |
| BLACKGANG CHINE, — | Hotel—Brooks. |
| NITON, — | Royal Sandrock Hotel—Kent. |
| | Boarding-house, on the shore—Bailey. |
| | White Lion, Niton village—Bright. |
| | Buddle Inn— |
| VENTNOR, — | Hotel—Riles. |
| | Marine Hotel—Bush. |
| | Crab and Lobster—Cass. |
| | Commercial Inn—Cummins. |
| BONCHURCH, — | Hotel—Ribbands. |
| SHANKLIN, — | Williams's Hotel—Hale. |
| | Hotel—Daish. |

| | |
|---|---|
| SANDOWN, — | King's-head — Thomas. |
| BEMBRIDGE, — | Hotel, on the beach — Fletcher. |
| BRADING, — | Wheat-sheaf — Lale. |
| CALBOURNE, — | Sun — Woodford. |
| GODSHILL, — | Griffin — Smith. |
| BRIXTON, — | New Inn — Sanders. |

## LIST OF THE PRINCIPAL
## SEATS & COUNTRY-VILLAS
## WITH THE NAMES OF

Their Proprietors or Occupiers.

☞ *In those instances where no Occupiers' Names appear, such Residences are generally to be sold or let.*

| | |
|---|---|
| OSBORNE, | Her Most Gracious Majesty the Queen |
| APPULDURCOMBE, | Earl Yarborough. |
| Afton Manor-house, | B. Cotton, esq. |
| Appley, near Ryde, | J. Hyde, esq. |
| Beauchamp, Undercliff, | Sir W. Gordon, bt. |
| Bellecroft, near Newport, | J. Cooke, esq. |
| Bembridge Parsonage, | Rev. F.G. Middleton. |
| Billingham, near Kingston | W. Stancombe, esq. |
| Binstead Cottage, | Lord Downes. |

| | |
|---|---|
| — — — Parsonage, | Rev. Philip Hewitt. |
| Blackwater Cottage, S. of Newport, | J. Rutherford, esq. |
| Brixton Parsonage, | Rev. E. McAll. |
| Brook Manor-house, | James How, esq. |
| Brookfield Cottage, Binstead, | Rev. Aug. Hewitt. |
| Calbourne Parsonage, | Rev. R. Sumner. |
| Castlehurst, nr. Carisbrooke, | H. Pinnock, esq. |
| Chale Parsonage, | Rev. A. Gother. |
| Costorphine-hill, Ryde, | J.P. Lind, esq. |
| EAST COWES CASTLE, | — — |
| East Dene, Bonchurch, | Capt. Swinburne. |
| Egypt House, nr. W. Cowes, | Sir T. Tancred, bt. |
| Elm Cottage, near E. Cowes, | — — |
| FAIRLEE, N.E. of Newport, | Rd. Oglander, esq. |
| Fairlee Cottage, ditto, | — — |
| Fairy-hill, Nettlestone, | W.A. Glynn, esq. |
| Farringford-hill, Freshwater, | Rev. G. Seymour. |
| FERNHILL, Wootton, | Samuel Sanders, esq. |
| GATCOMBE PARK, | Captain Berners. |
| Gatcombe Rectory, | Rev. W. Thompson, D.D. |
| Hampstead, near Shalfleet, | Mrs. Nash. |
| Haylands, south of Ryde, | Captain Locke. |
| Hill-grove, Bembridge, | Hon. A.H. Moreton. |
| Holmwood, Ryde, | T.B. Maynard, esq. |
| Kite-hill, Wootton, | Sir H. Brook, bt. |
| Lowcliff Lodge, Blackgang, | — — |
| Mill-hill, West Cowes, | — — |
| Medina Hermitage, nr. Niton, | W.H. Dawes, esq. |
| Mirables, Undercliff, ditto, | Mrs. Arnold. |
| Mount Cleeves House, ditto, | the Misses Simes. |
| Moor House, near W. Cowes, | — — |

| | |
|---|---|
| Mottistone House, | R. Jessett, esq. |
| New Close, s.w. of Newport, | T. Cooke, esq. |
| Ningwood House, | Rev. —— Cottell. |
| Niton Parsonage, | Rev. R. Dixon. |
| NORRIS, near E. Cowes, | R. Bell, esq. |
| NORTHCOURT, Shorwell, | H.P. Gordon, esq. |
| Shide Cottage, S. of Newport, | Col. Napier. |
| NORTHWOOD PARK, | G.H. Ward, esq. |
| Norton Lodge, Freshwater, | Sir G. Hamond, bt. |
| NUNWELL, near Brading, | Sir W. Oglander, bt. |
| Oakhill, near Ryde, | T.M. Leacock, esq. |
| Old Park, Undercliff, | J. Walkinshaw, esq. |
| Orchard, ditto, near Niton, | Sir W. Gordon, bt. |
| Padmore, Whippingham, | Rev. James Jolliffe. |
| Pidford, near Rookley, | —— |
| Pitt-place, Mottistone, | —— |
| PRIORY, N. of St. Helen's, | H. Smith, esq. |
| Puckaster Cottage, Undercliff, | Mrs. Vine. |
| Puckpool, east of Ryde, | Lewis Wyatt, esq. |
| Ryde House, | Miss Player. |
| Rookley Cottage, | John Woodward, esq. |
| Rosiere, Niton, | —— |
| Sealand Cottage, Blackgang, | R. Pinnock, esq. |
| St. Clare, east of Ryde, | Col. Vernon Harcourt. |
| ST. JOHN'S, ditto, | A.F. Hamilton, esq. |
| St. Lawrence Villa, | Earl Yarborough. |
| ——— Cottage, | Hon. Capt. D. Pelham. |
| St. Thomas' Villa, E. Cowes, | Miss Barrington. |
| Sea-grove, Nettlestone, | W. Gardiner esq. |
| Sea-field, ditto, | Henry Beach, esq. |
| Spring-field, ditto, | John Callender, esq. |
| Steane Villa, Bembridge, | —— |

| | |
|---|---|
| Shanklin Parsonage, | Archdeacon Hill. |
| Shorwell Parsonage, | Rev. E. Robertson. |
| Slatwoods, near East Cowes, | Miss Shedden. |
| Southlands House, Blackgang, | — — |
| Spring-hill, ditto, | George Shedden, esq. |
| Standen, south of Newport, | General Evelegh. |
| STEEPHILL CASTLE, | J. Hambrough, esq. |
| Stickworth, south of Arreton, | Mrs. Bell. |
| Stonepits' Cottage, Binstead, | Capt. Brigstocke. |
| SWAINSTON, nr. Calbourne, | Sir Rd. Simeon, bt. |
| The Battery, Sandown, | T. Woodham, esq. |
| The Farm, nr. Newport, | B. Mew, esq. |
| The Marina, Norton, | Capt. Crozier. |
| Tower Cottage, Shanklin, | — Cameron, esq. |
| Uplands, east of Ryde, | C. Payne, esq. |
| Upton House, south of Ryde, | Admiral Hoare. |
| Wacklands, s. of Newchurch, | William Thatcher, esq. |
| WESTOVER, Calbourne, | Hon. A'Court Holmes. |
| Westhill, Cowes, | the Misses Ward. |
| — — — Norton, | R.B. Crozier, esq. |
| Westcliff, Niton, | Captain Ker. |
| Westridge, east of Ryde, | Mrs. Young. |
| Westbrook, ditto, | J. Le Marchant, esq. |
| Whitcomb, near Gatcombe, | Mrs. Hughes. |
| Woodlands, east of Ryde, | J. Percival, esq. |
| Woodvale, near Gurnard | Captain Ffarington. |
| Wootton Parsonage. | Rev. R.W. White. |
| Yafford, near Shorwell, | James Jolliffe, esq. |
| Yaverland Parsonage, | Rev. R. Sherson. |

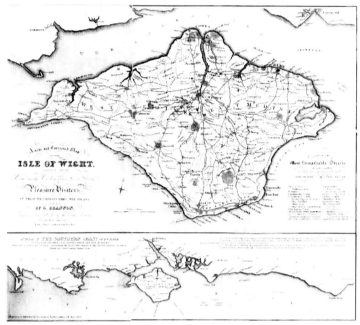

Map of the Isle of Wight

Lightning Source UK Ltd.
Milton Keynes UK
UKOW04f1829271114

242300UK00001B/116/P